book of

SHIRTLESS MEN

STEV PETER

For everybody who likes shirtless men!
And who not like? ;-)

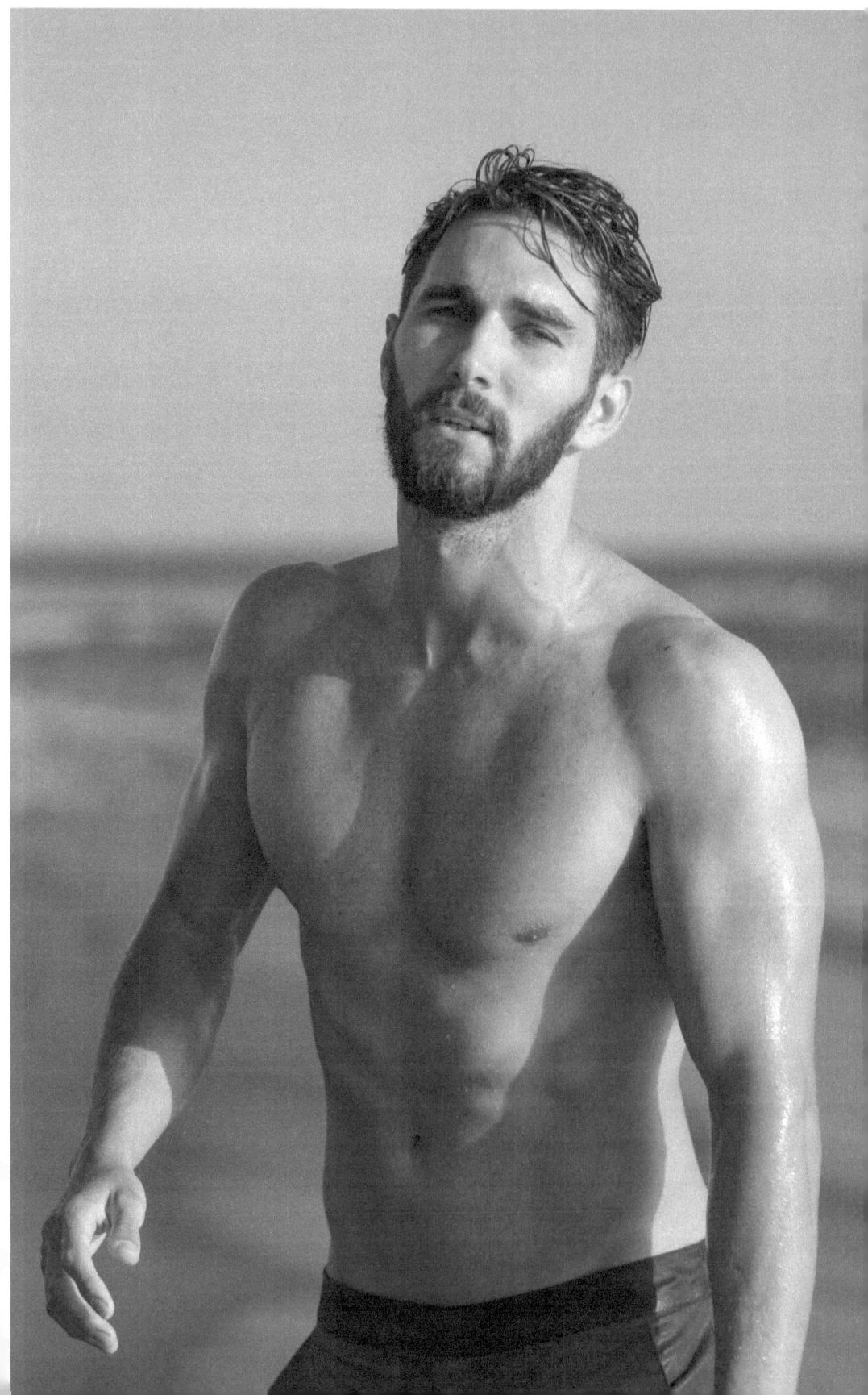

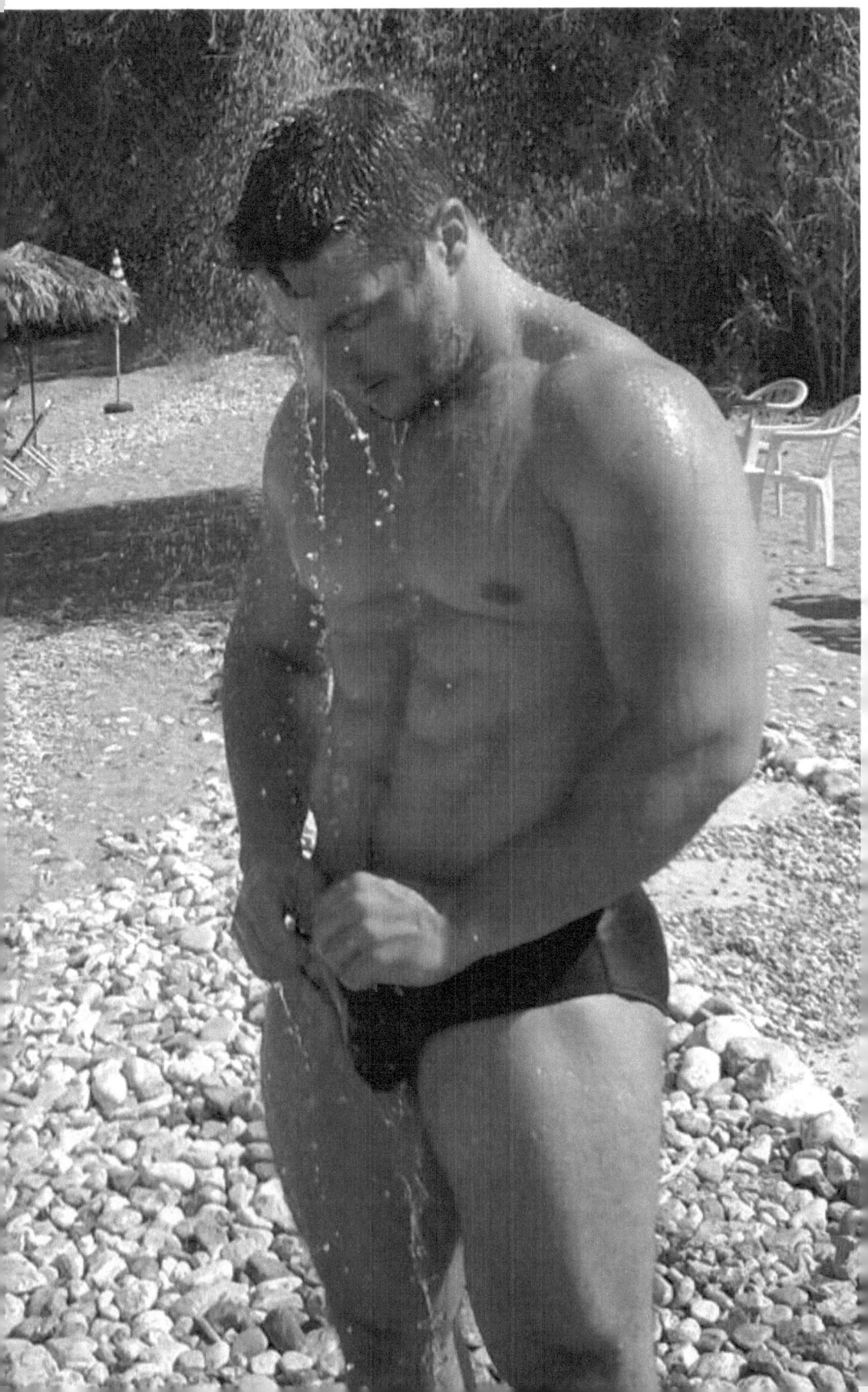

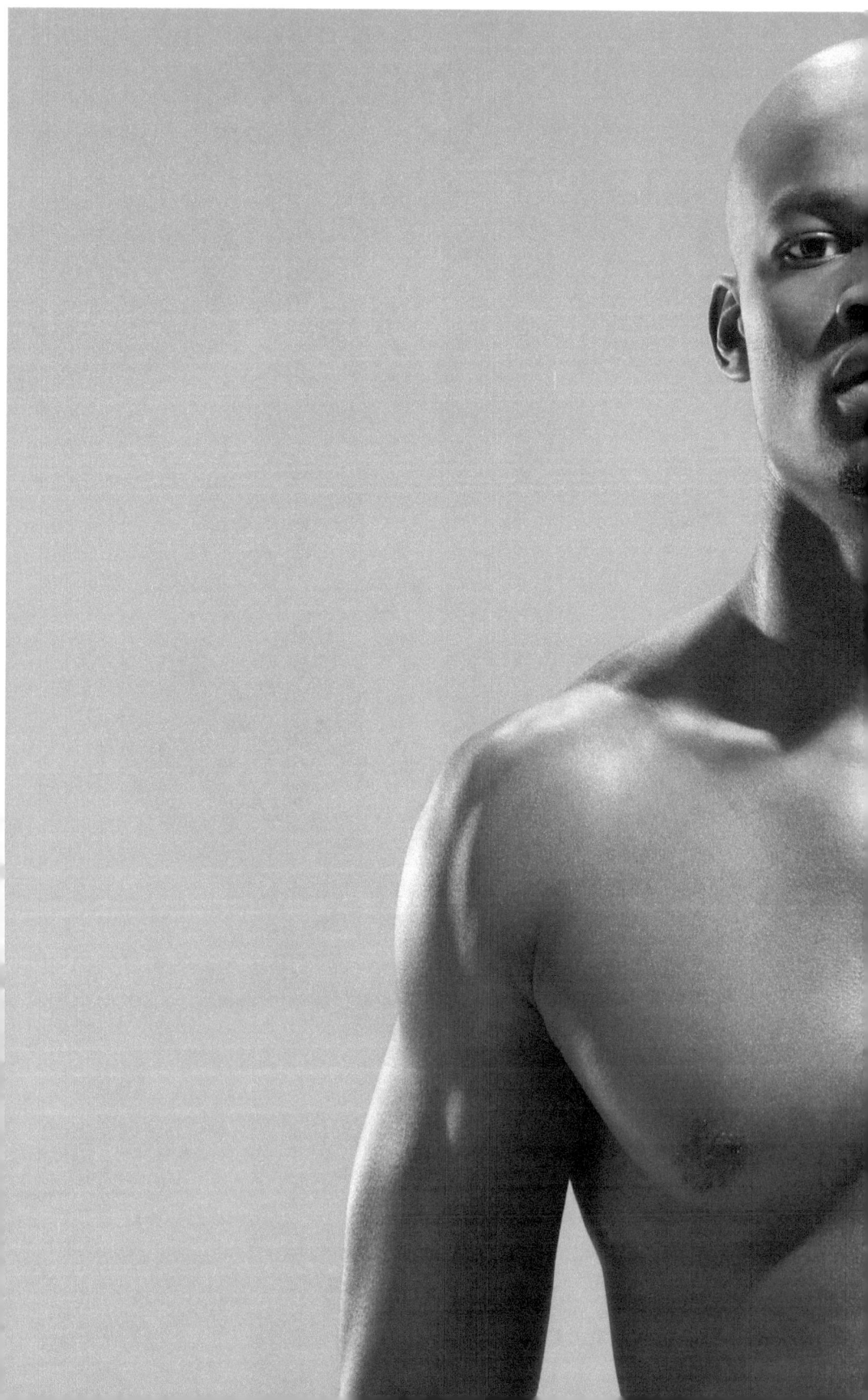

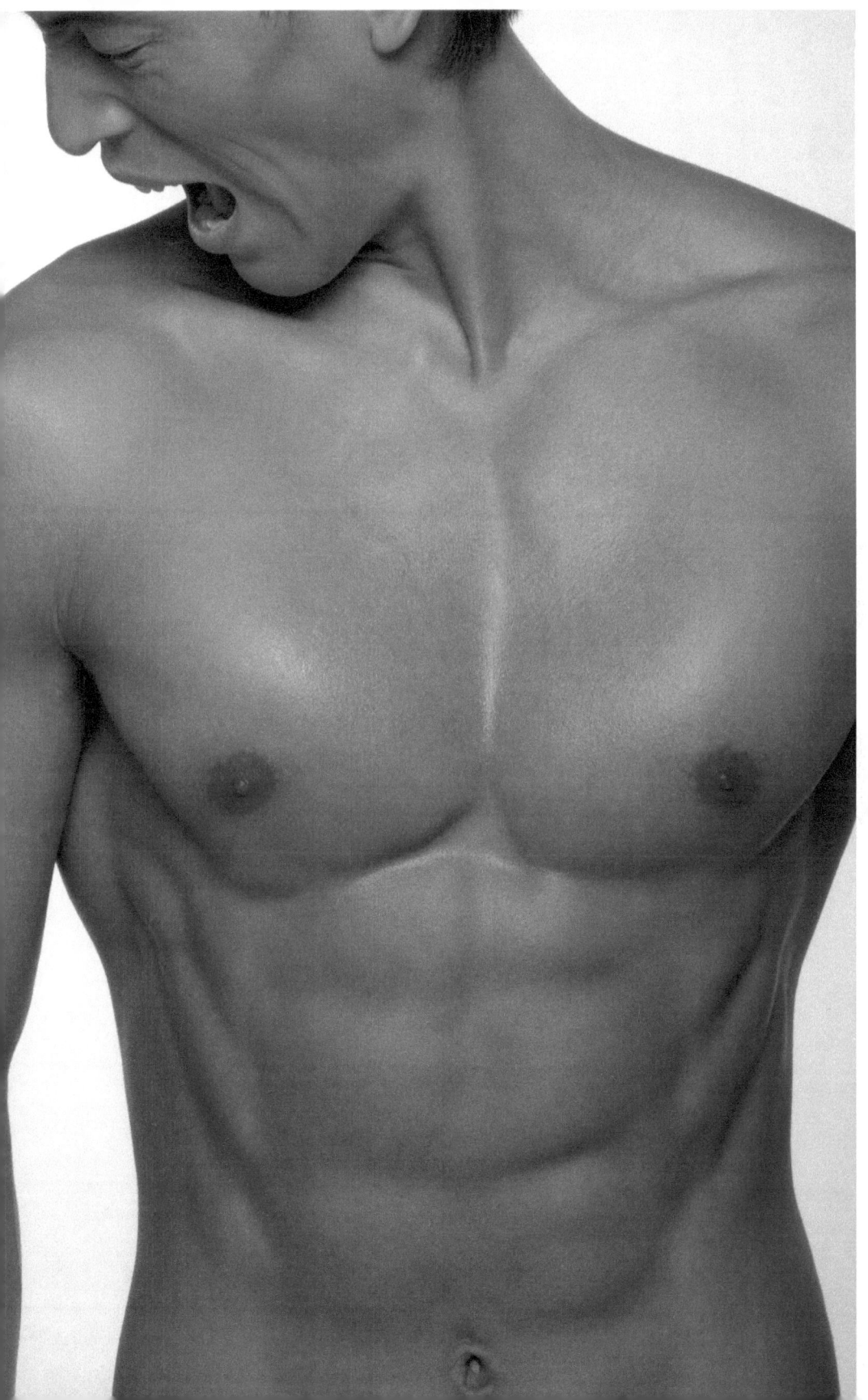

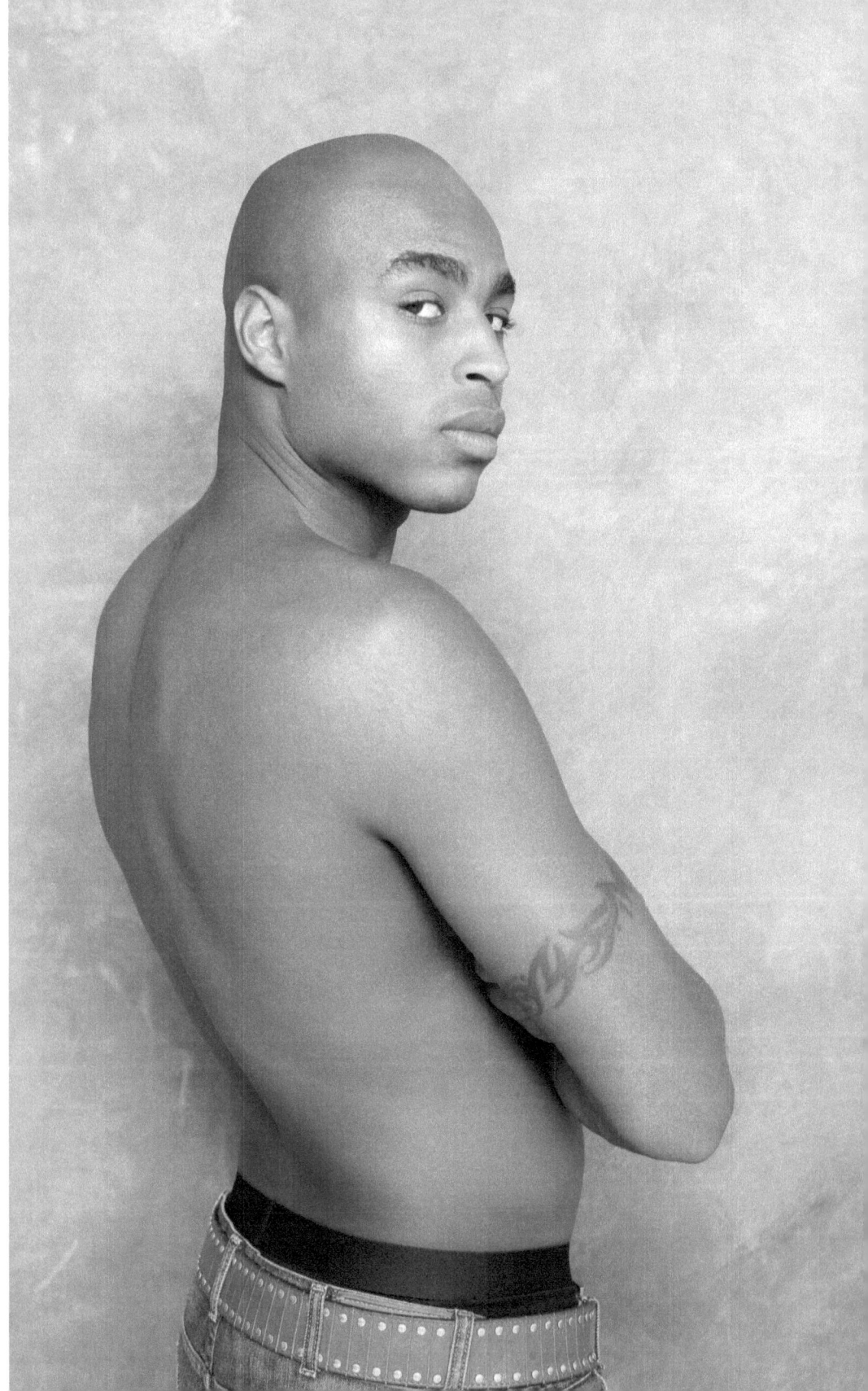

"I can be shy, but I'm not shy with my body. Everyone is naked under their clothes - so what?"

Cameron Richardson

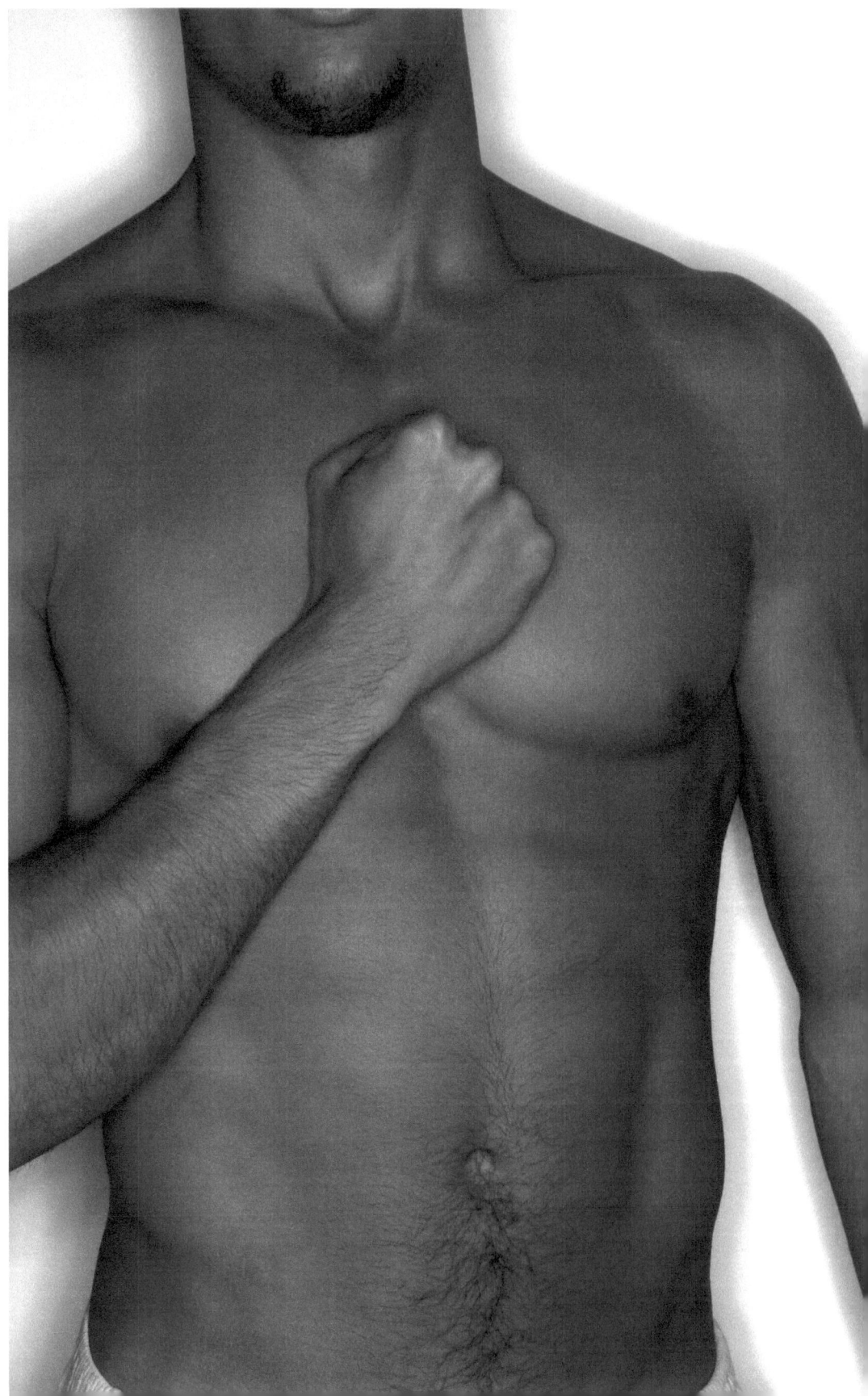

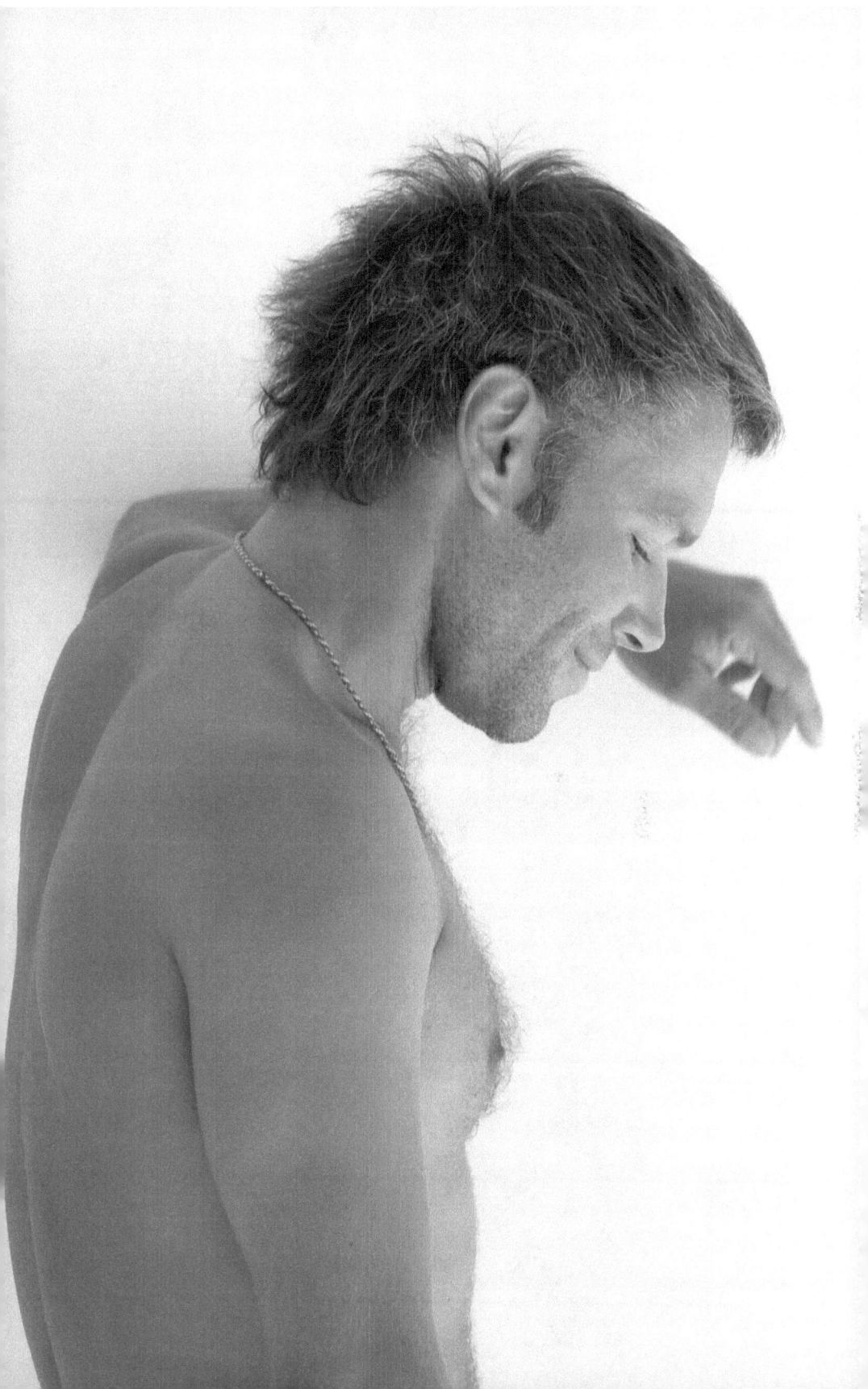

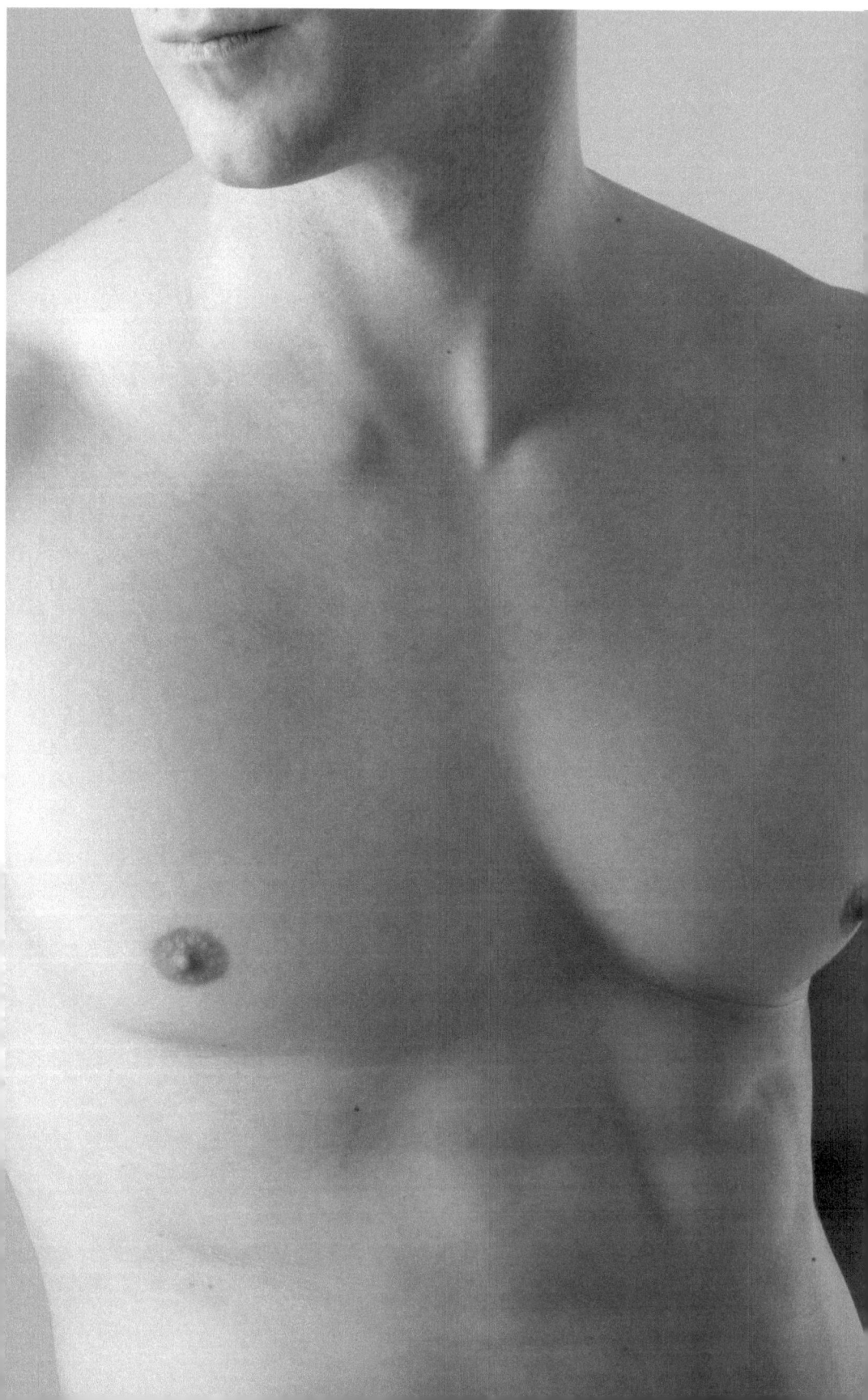

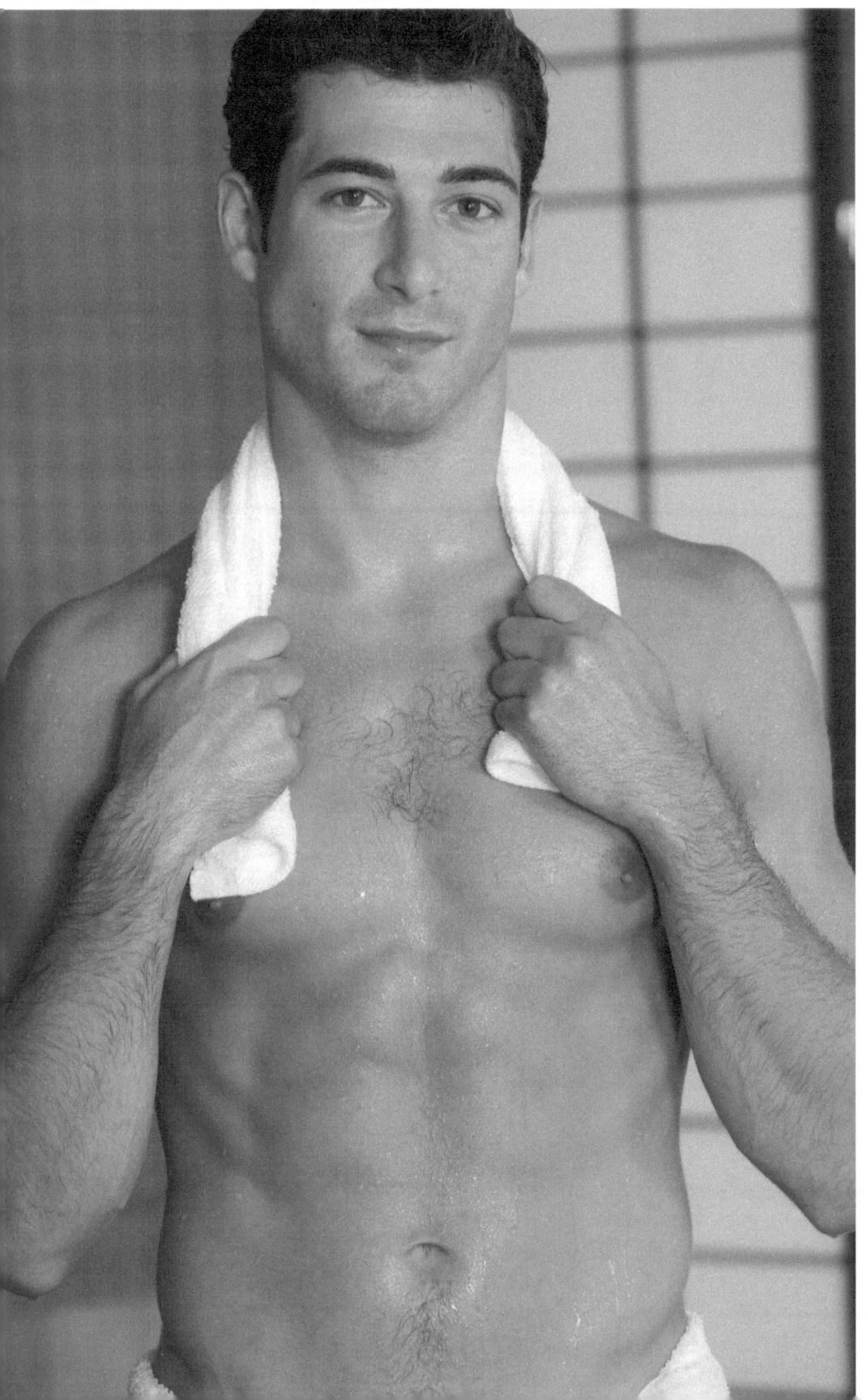

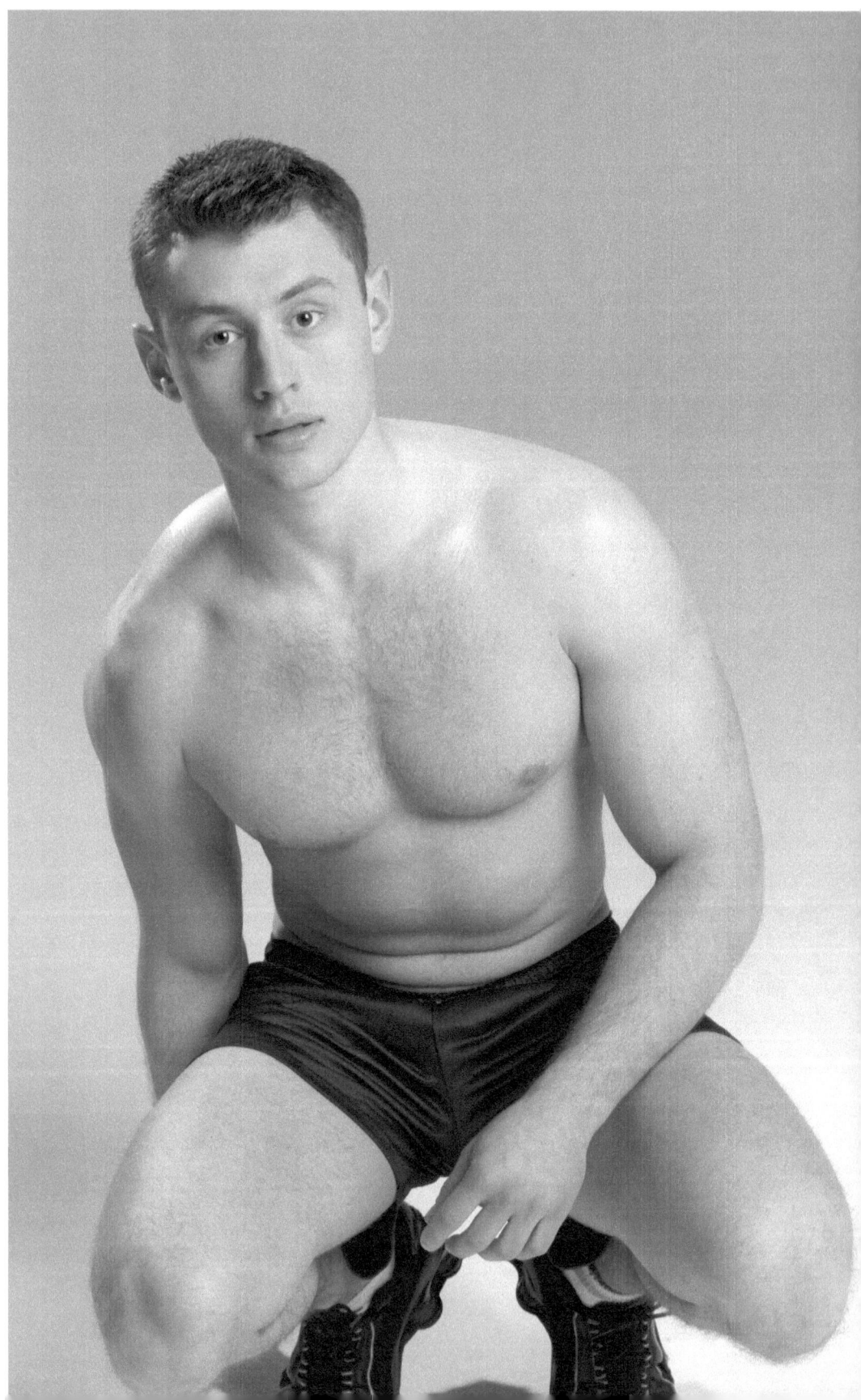

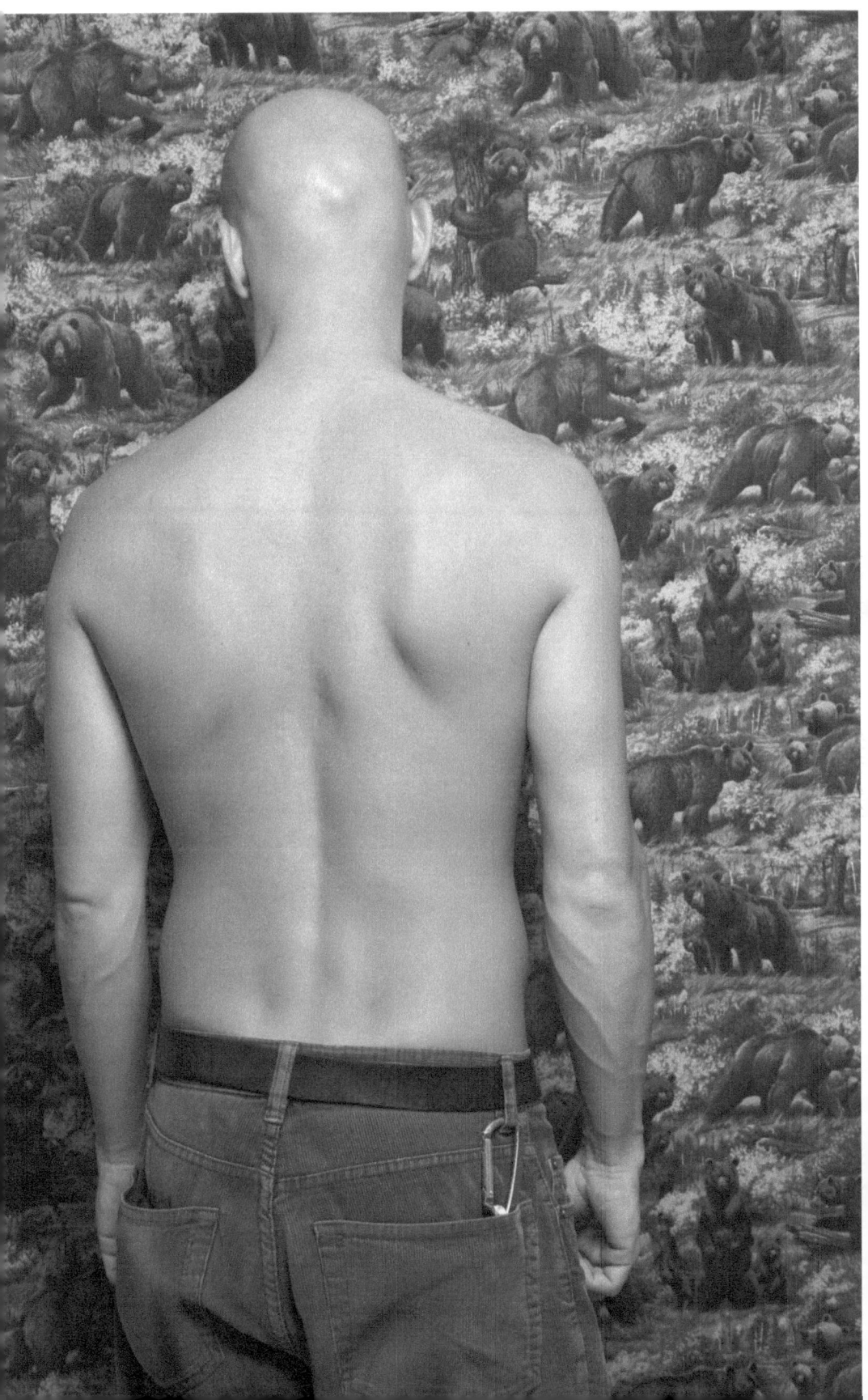

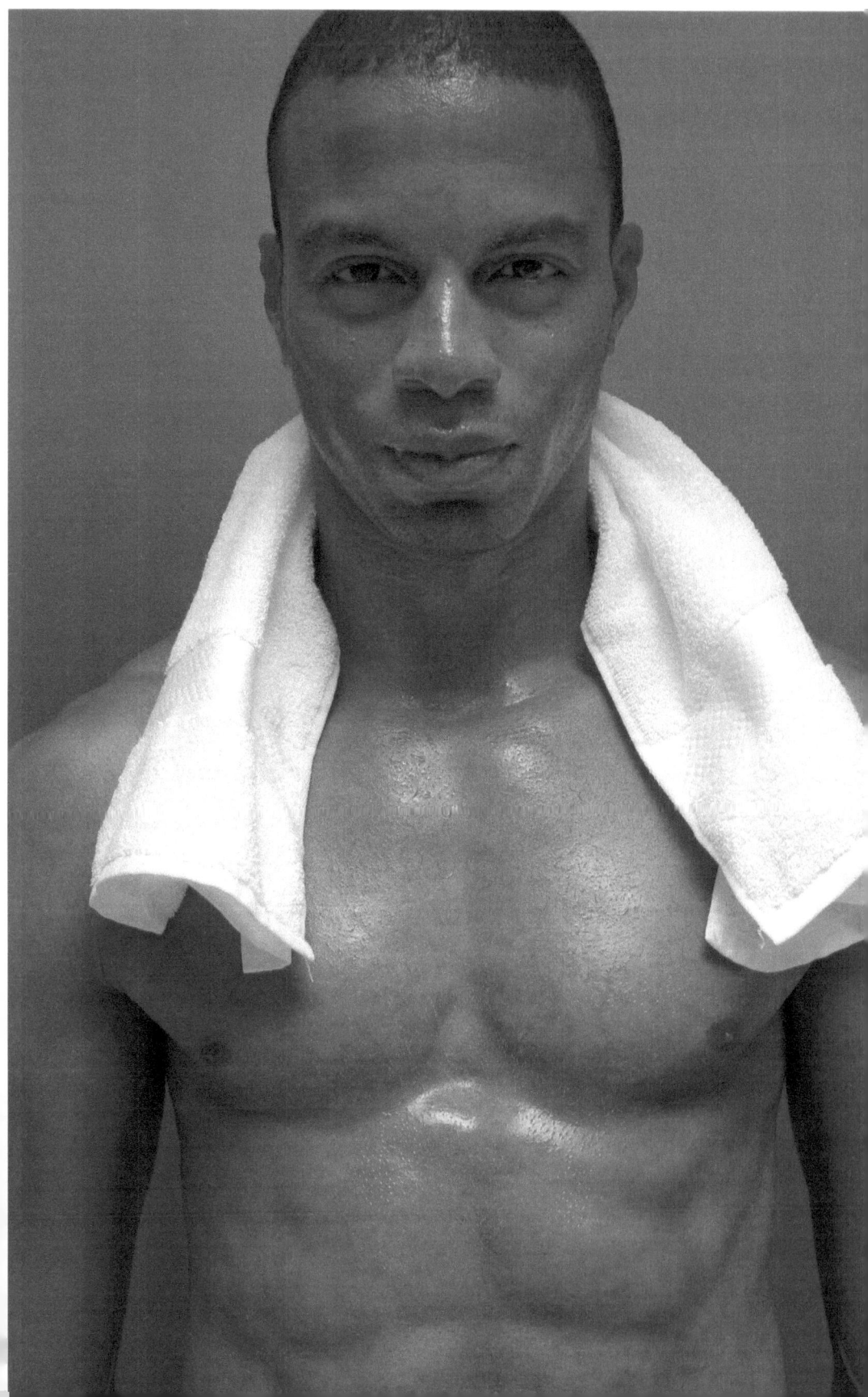

"I always say: To be well dressed you must be well naked."

Oscar de la Renta

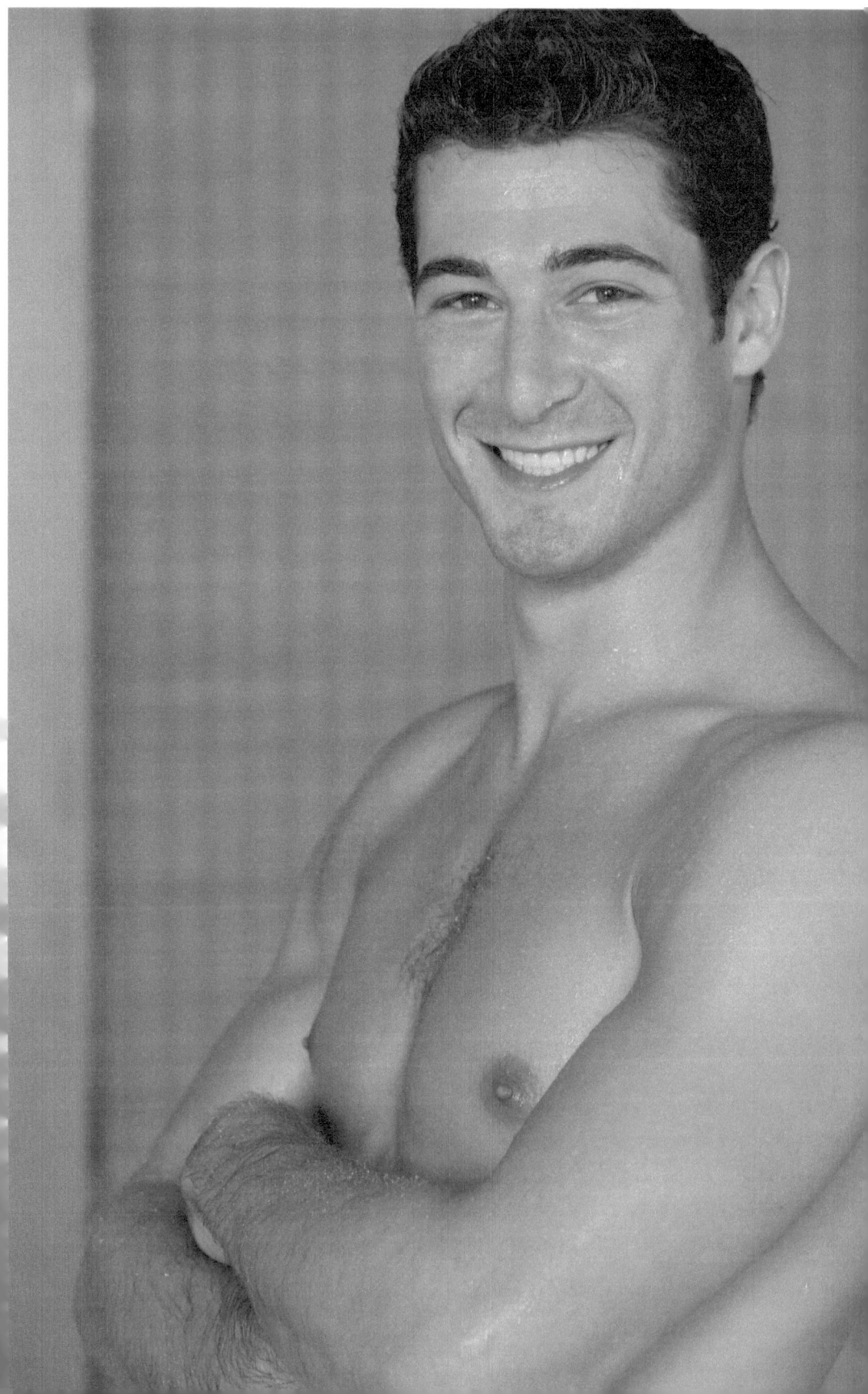

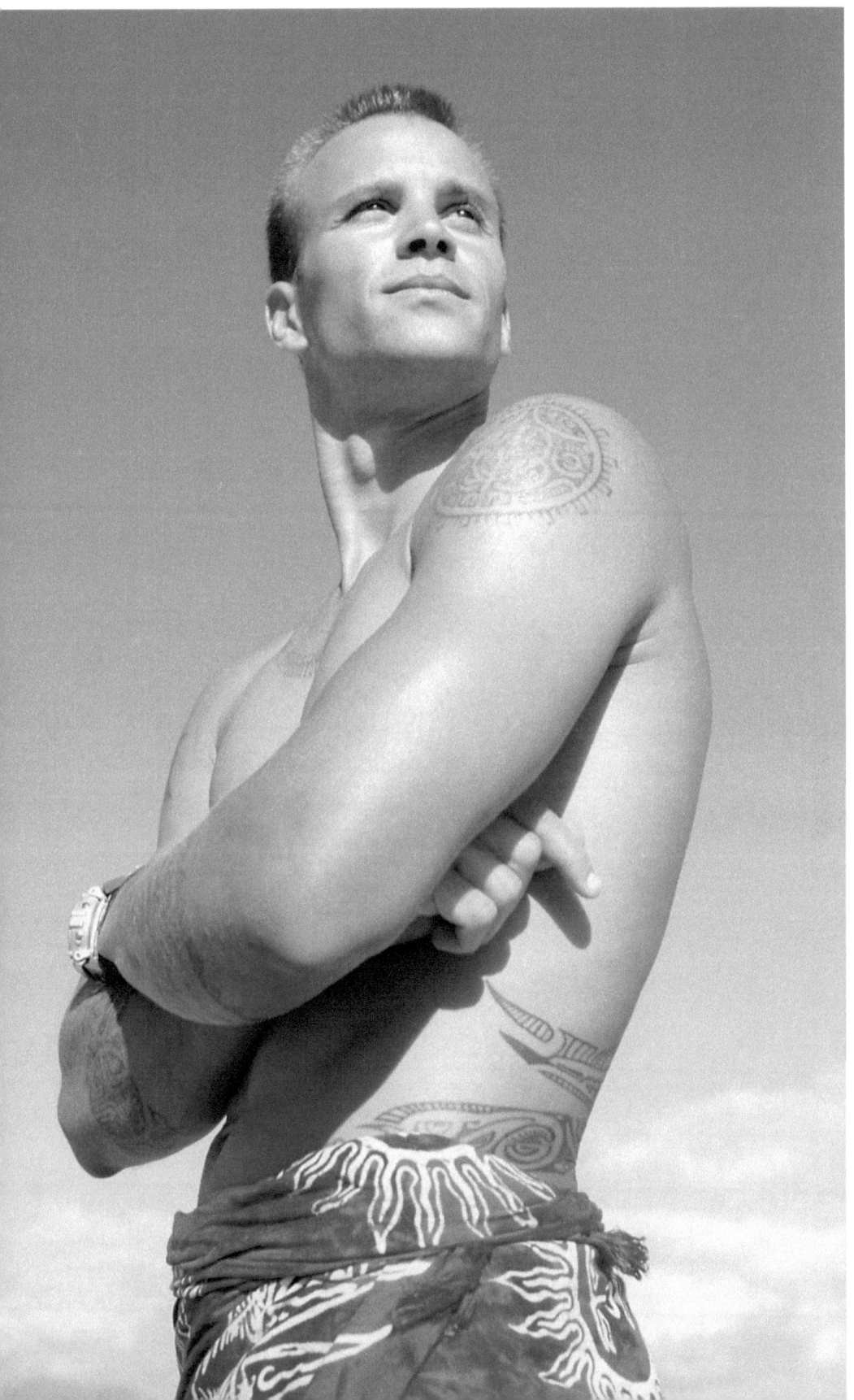

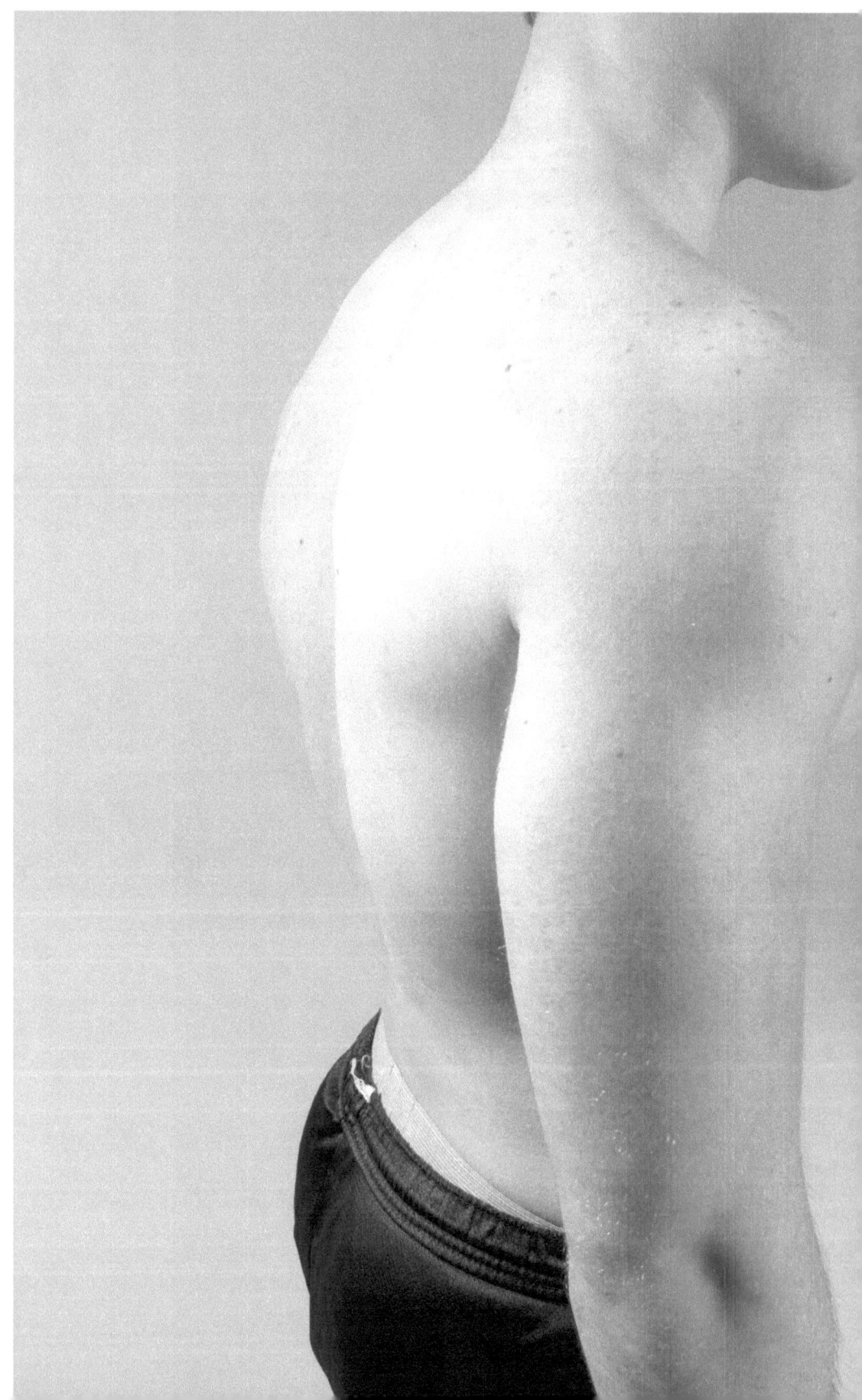

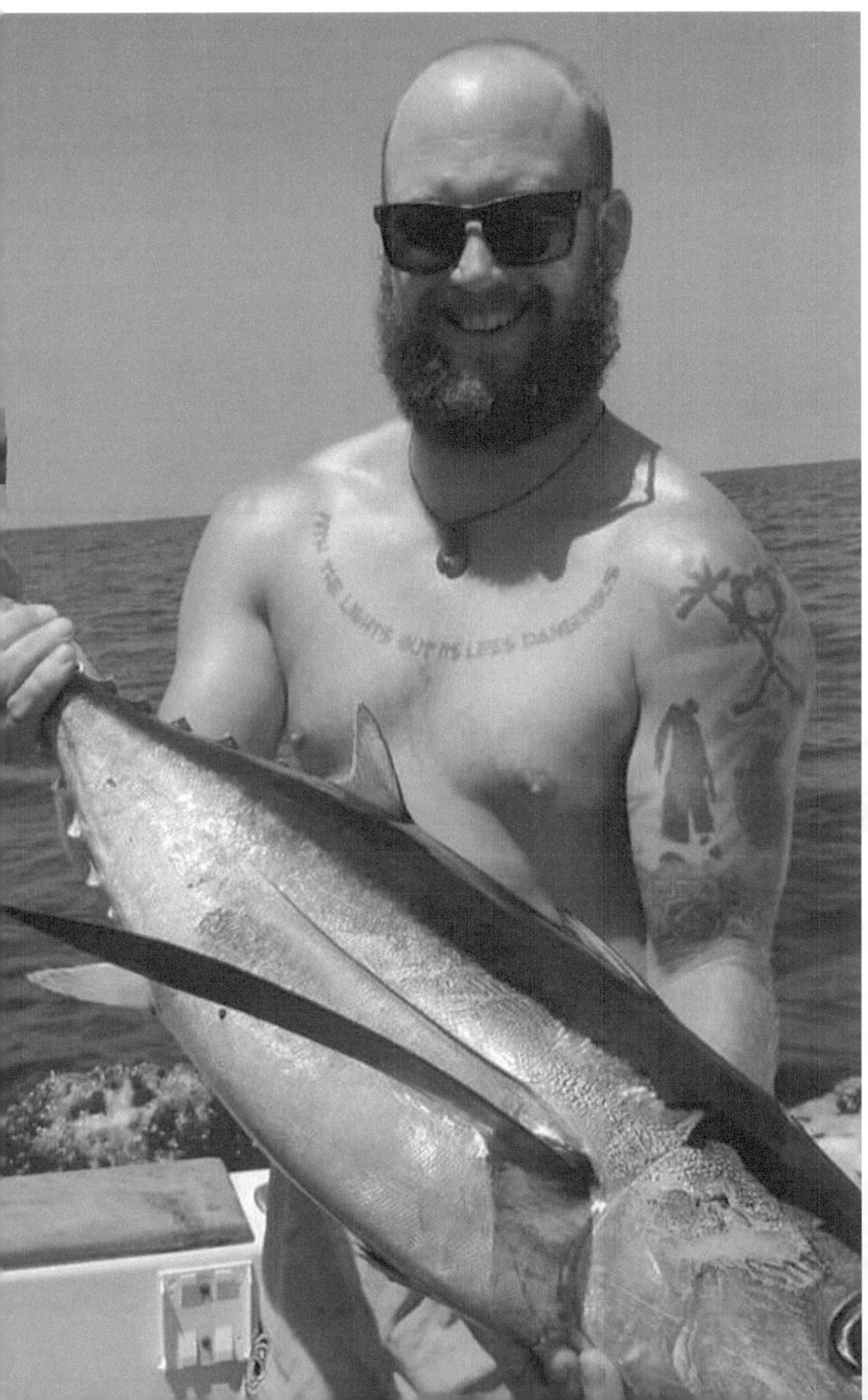

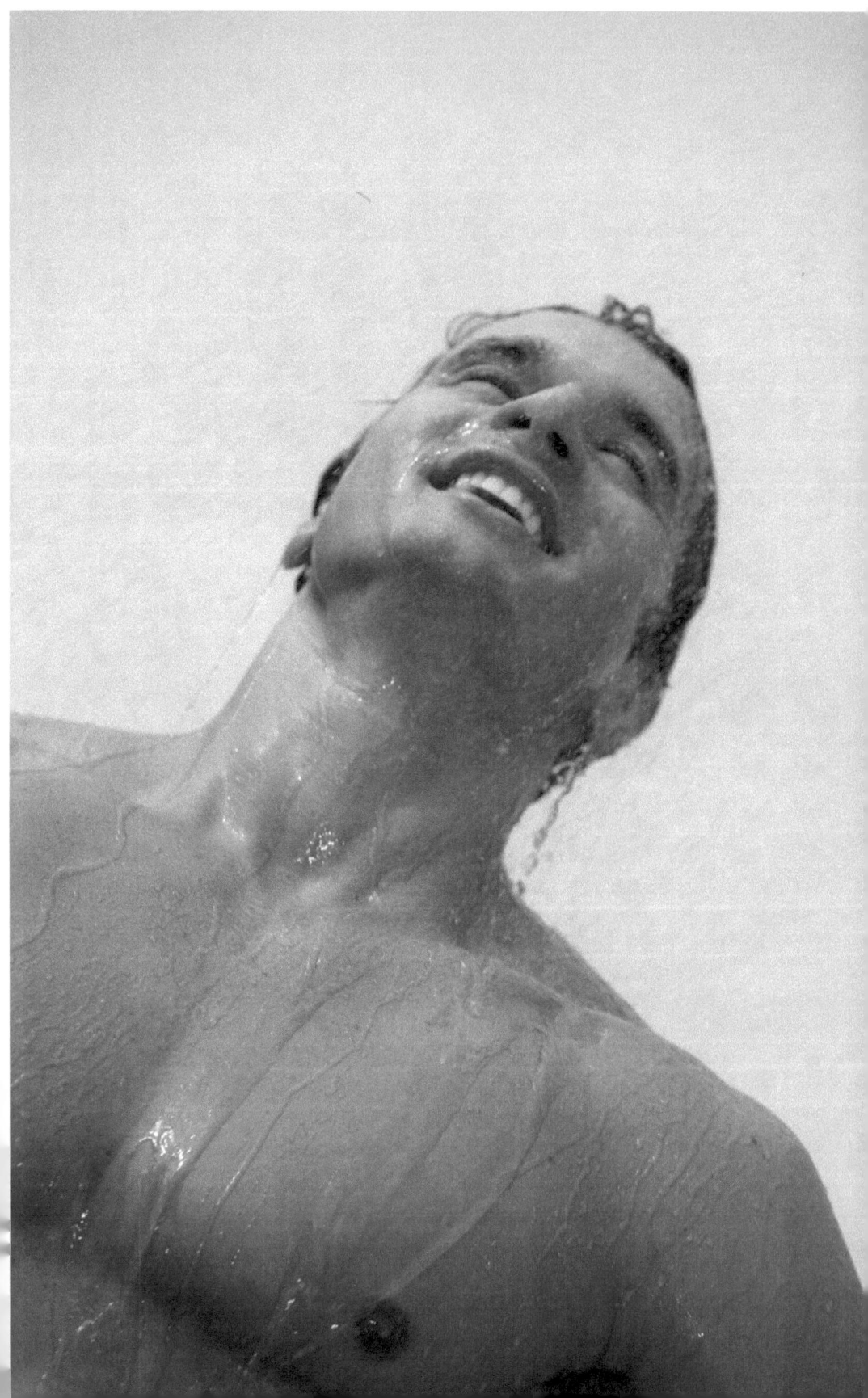

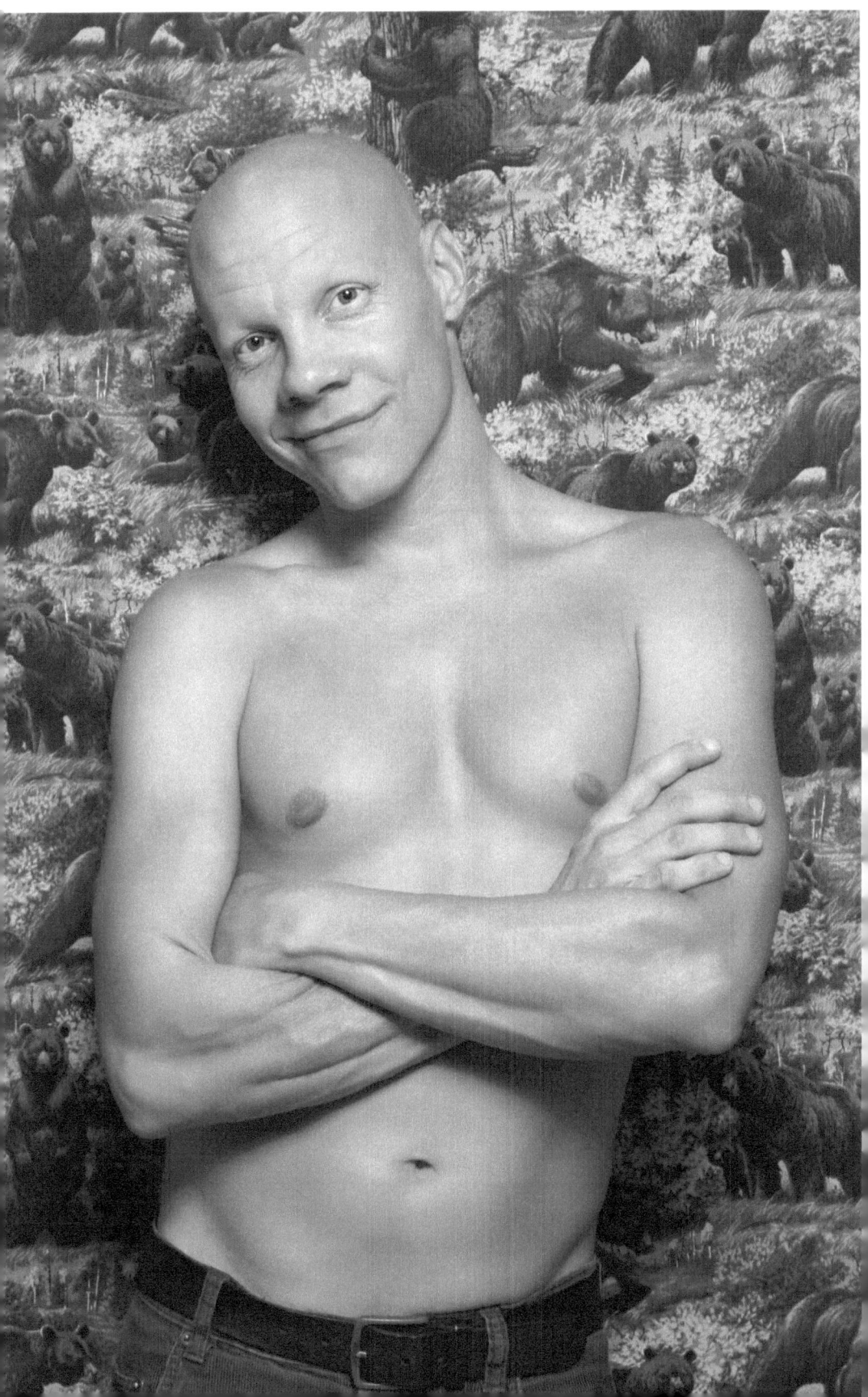

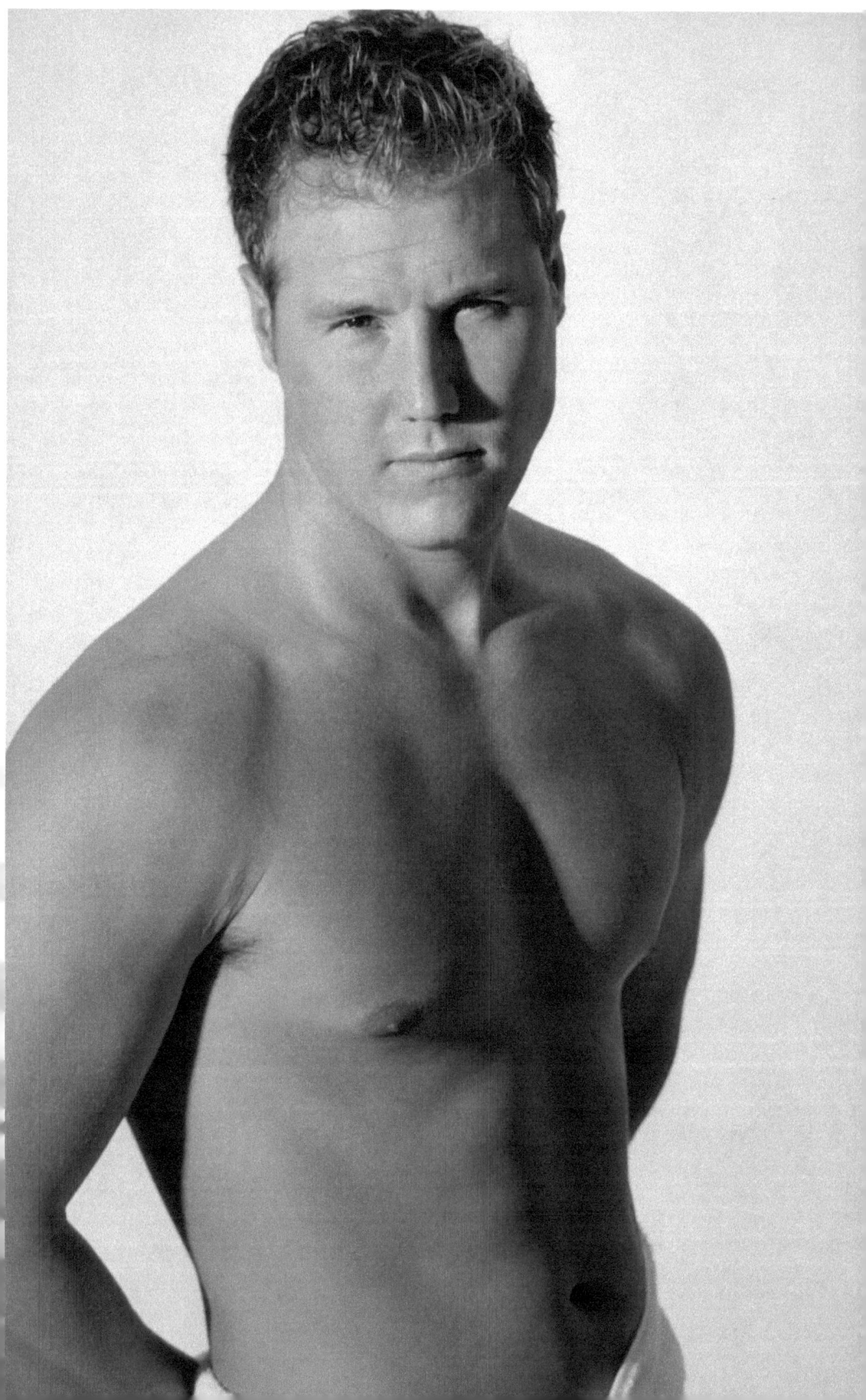

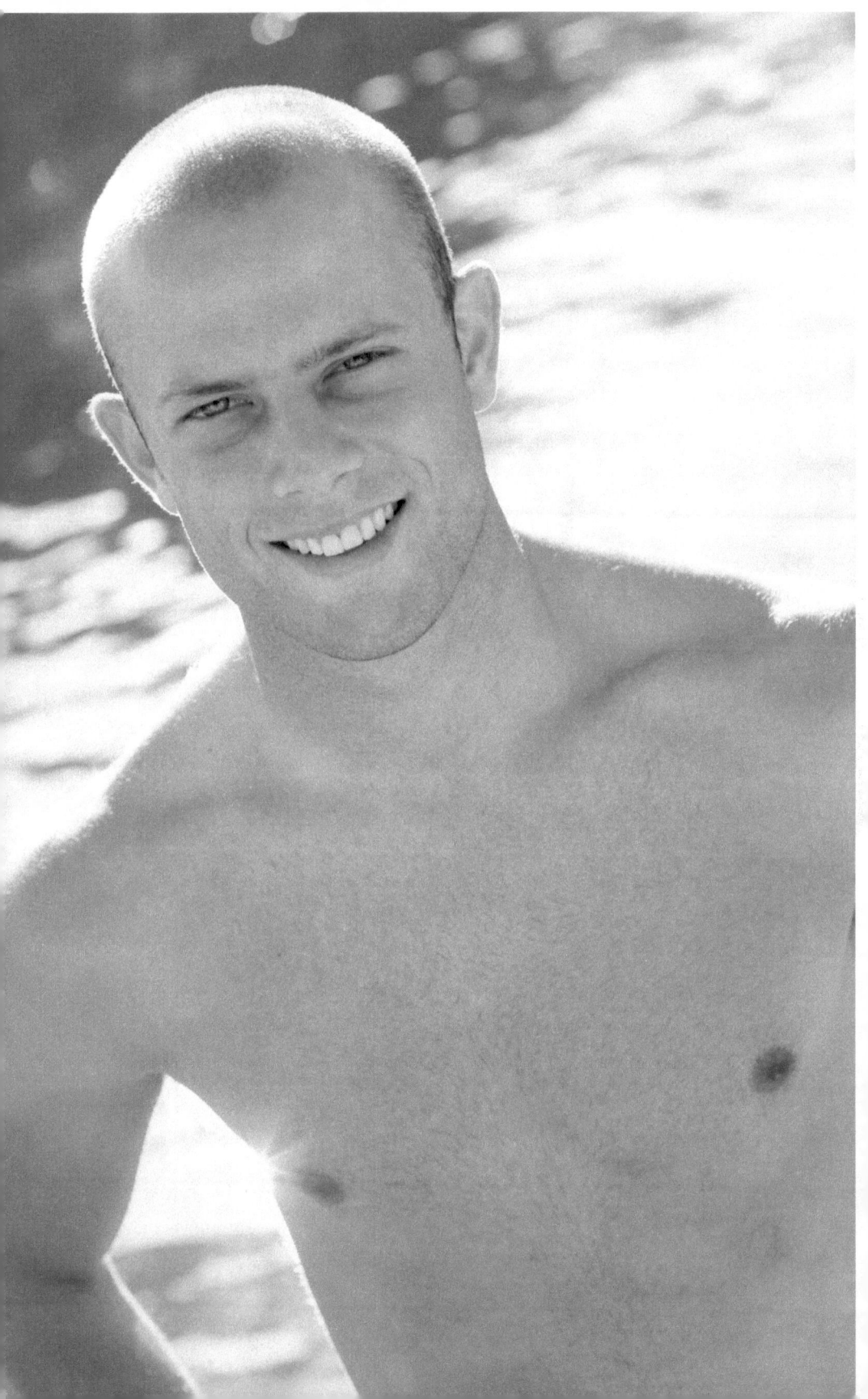

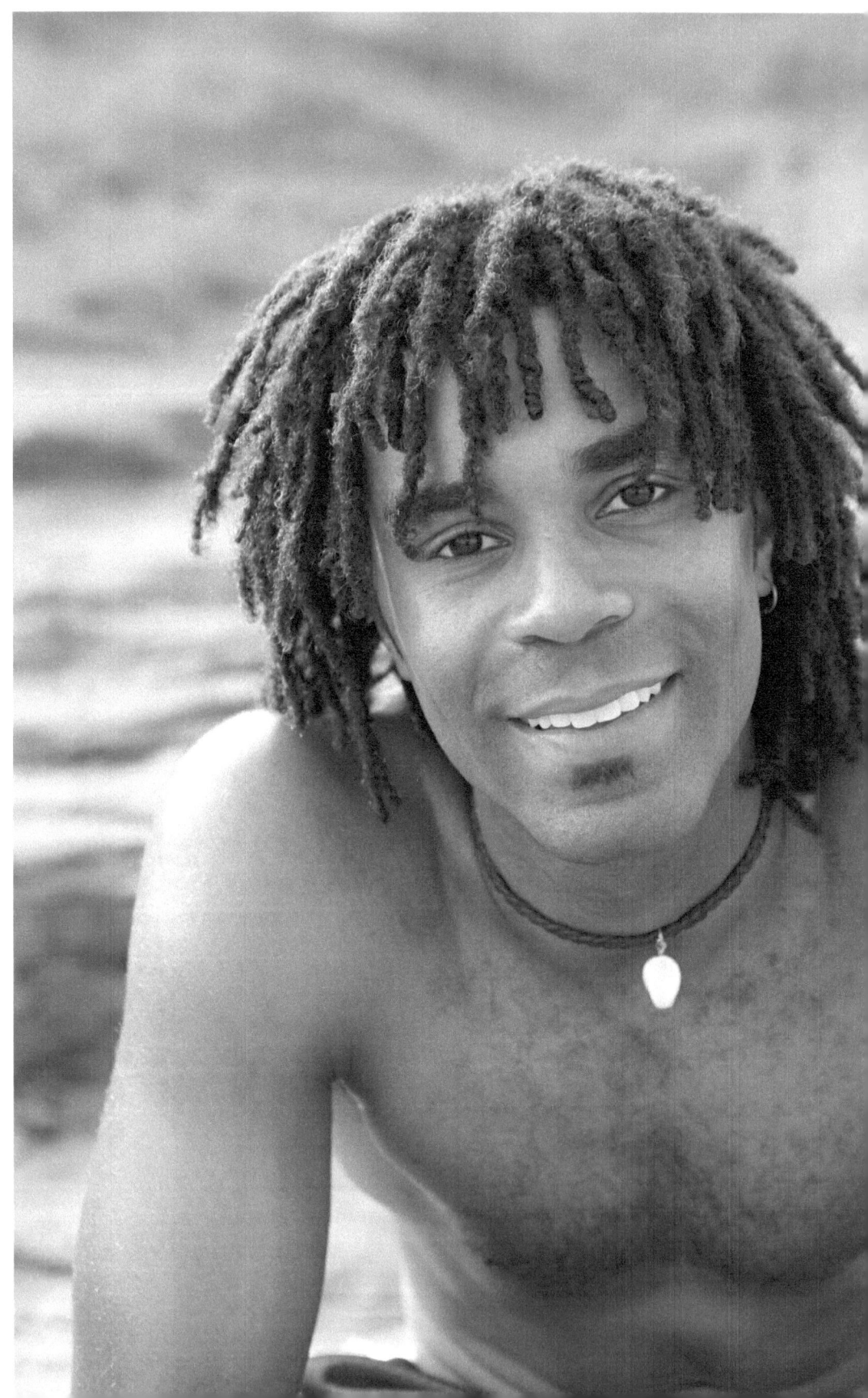

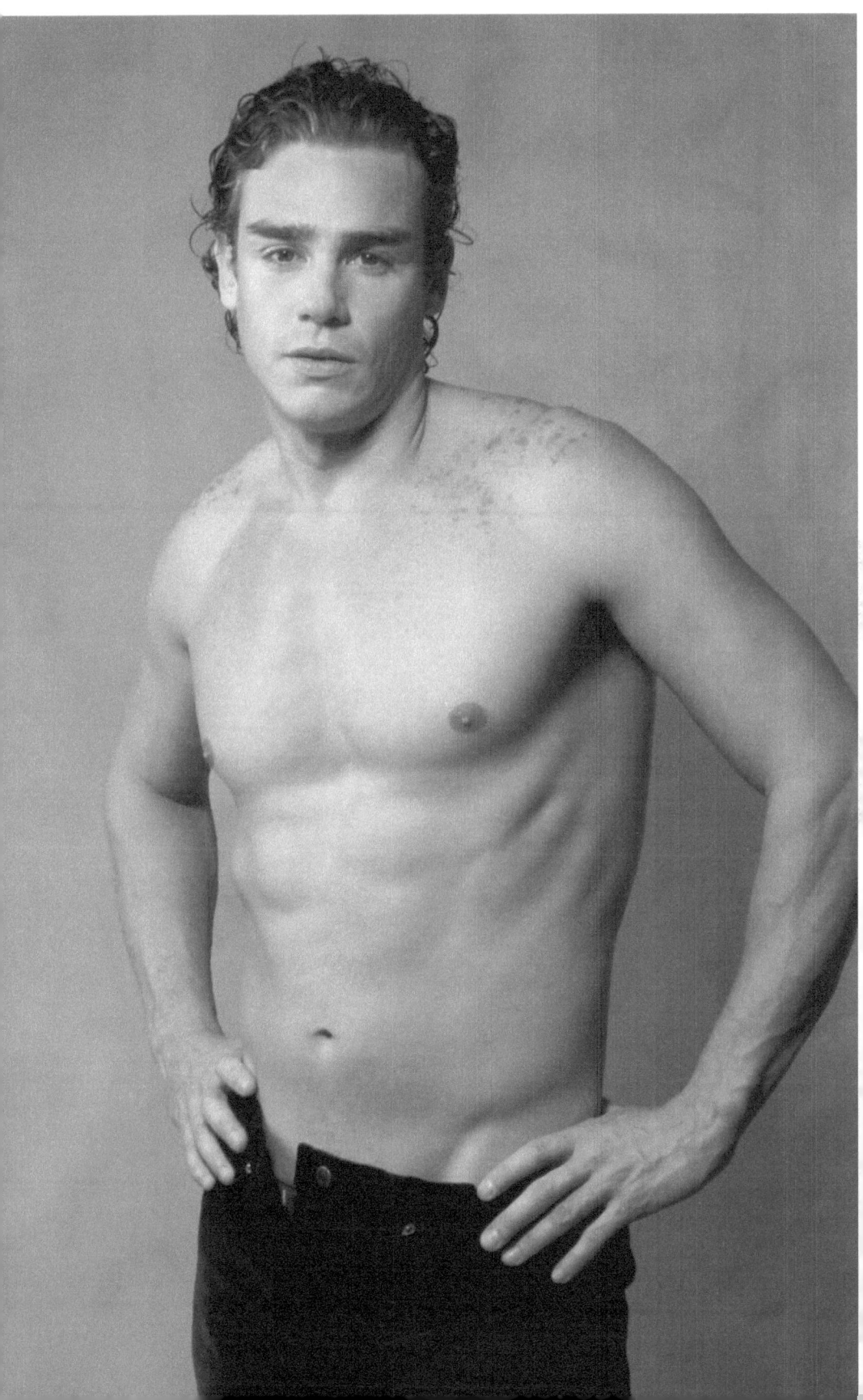

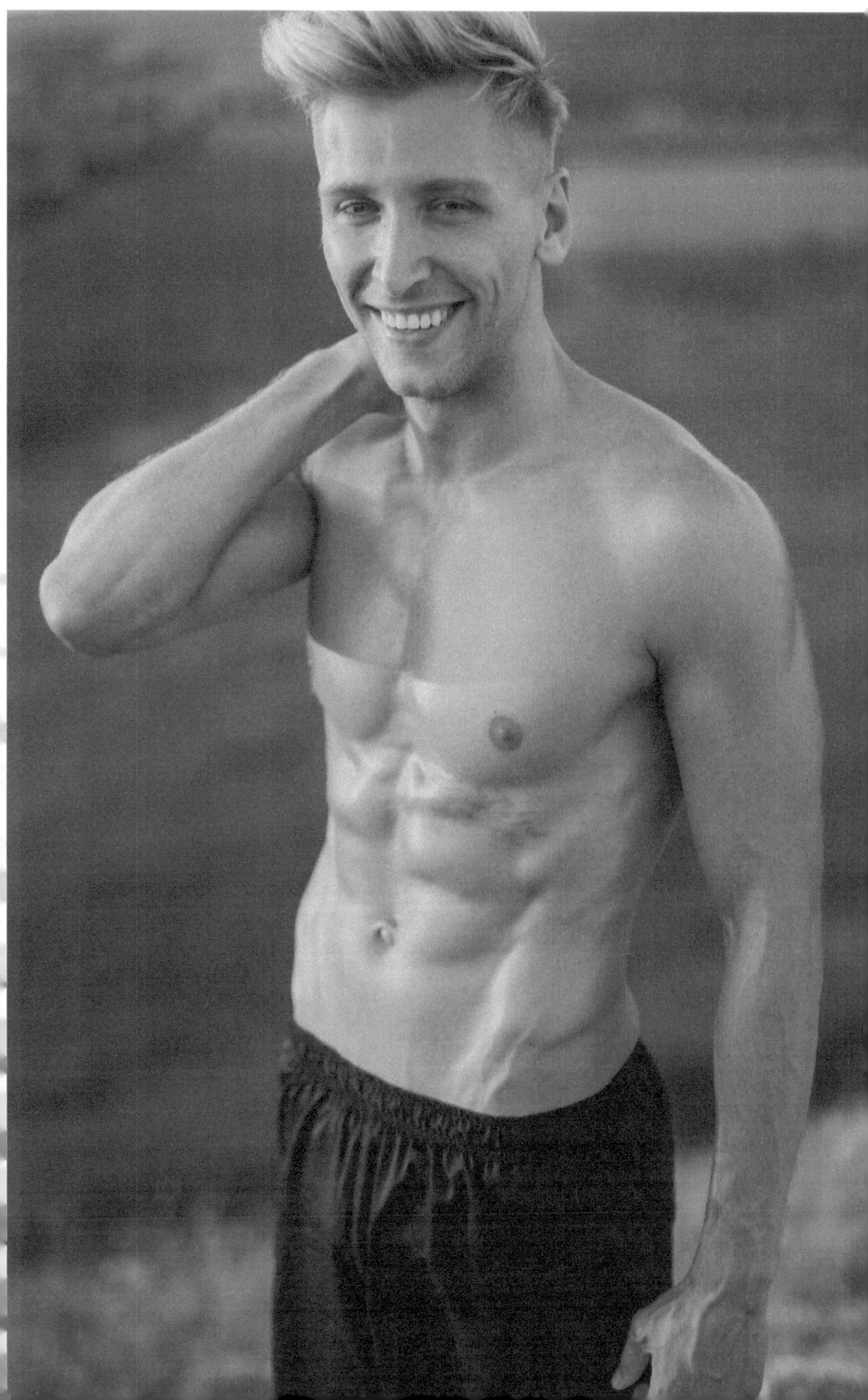

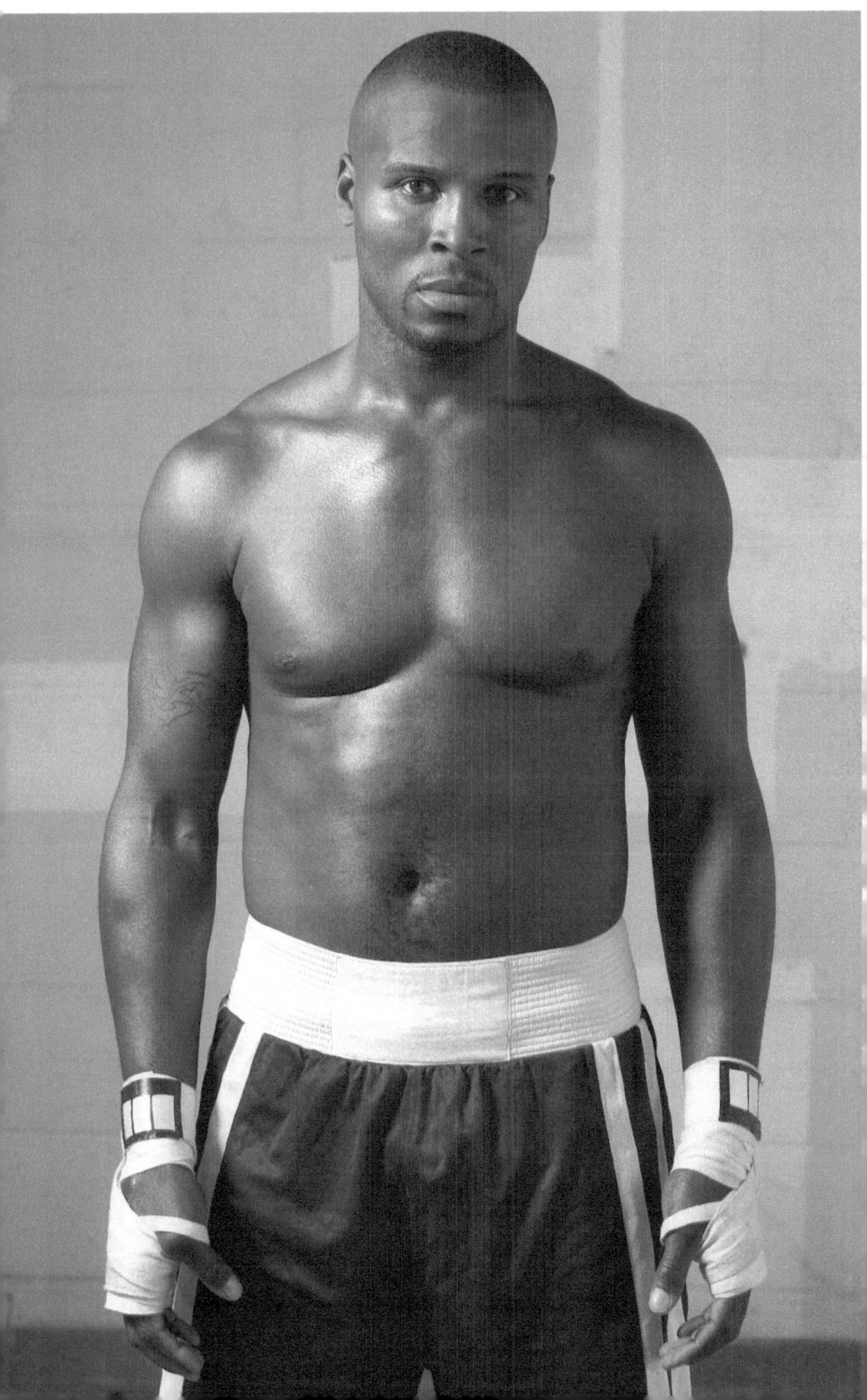

"If you look at sculptures from hundreds of years ago, everyone's naked. It's not a bad thing."

Gigi Hadid

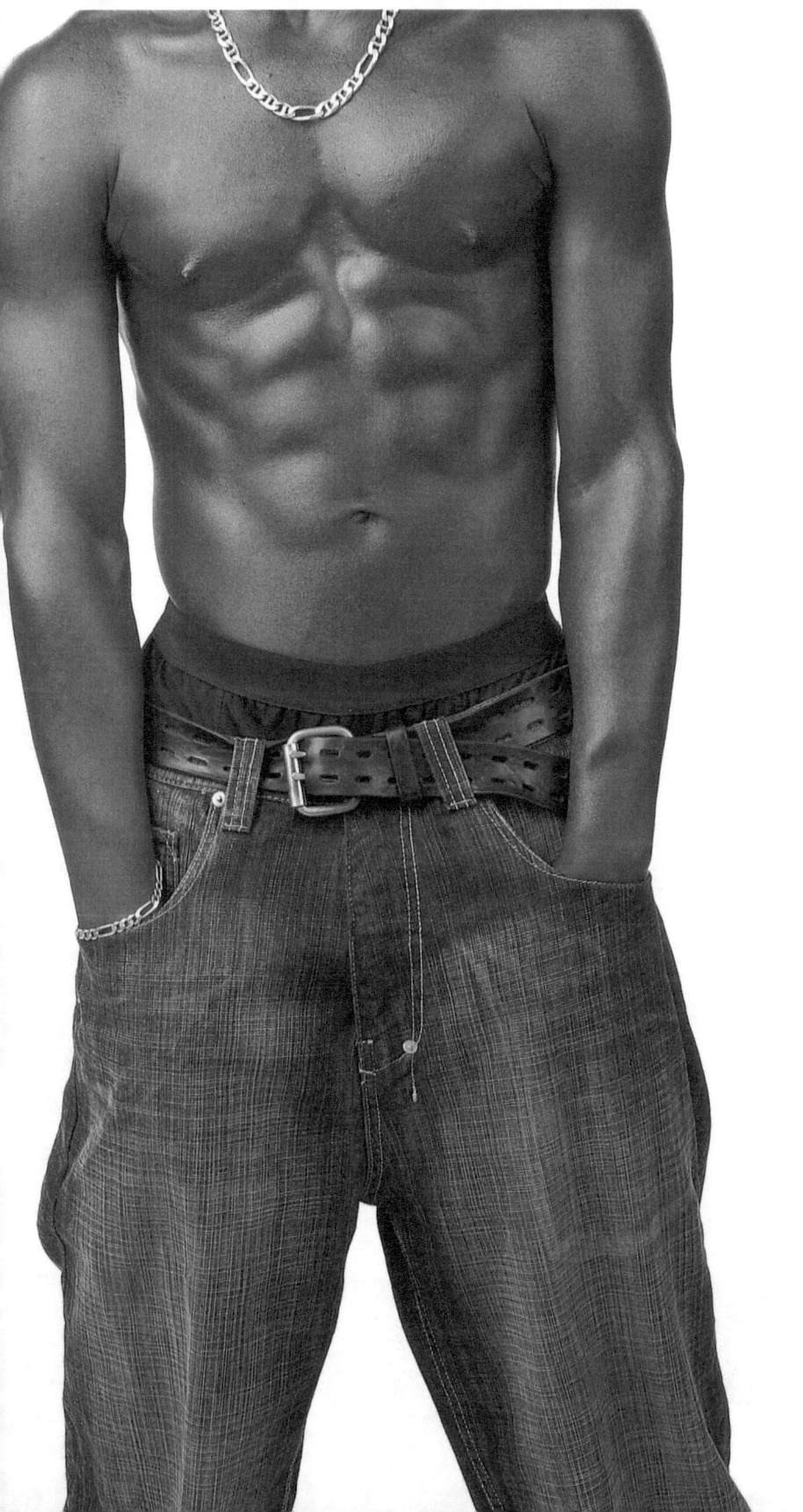

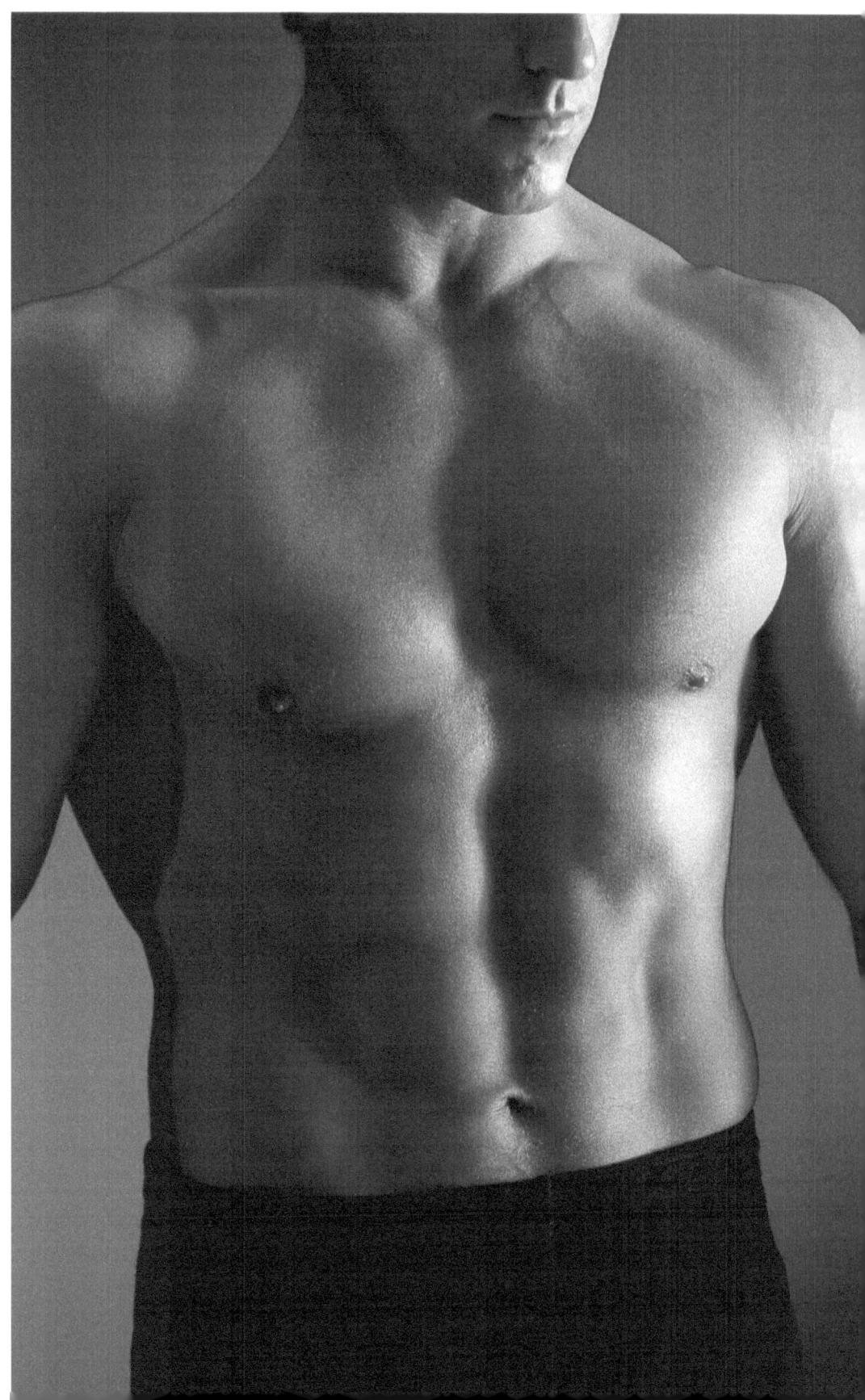

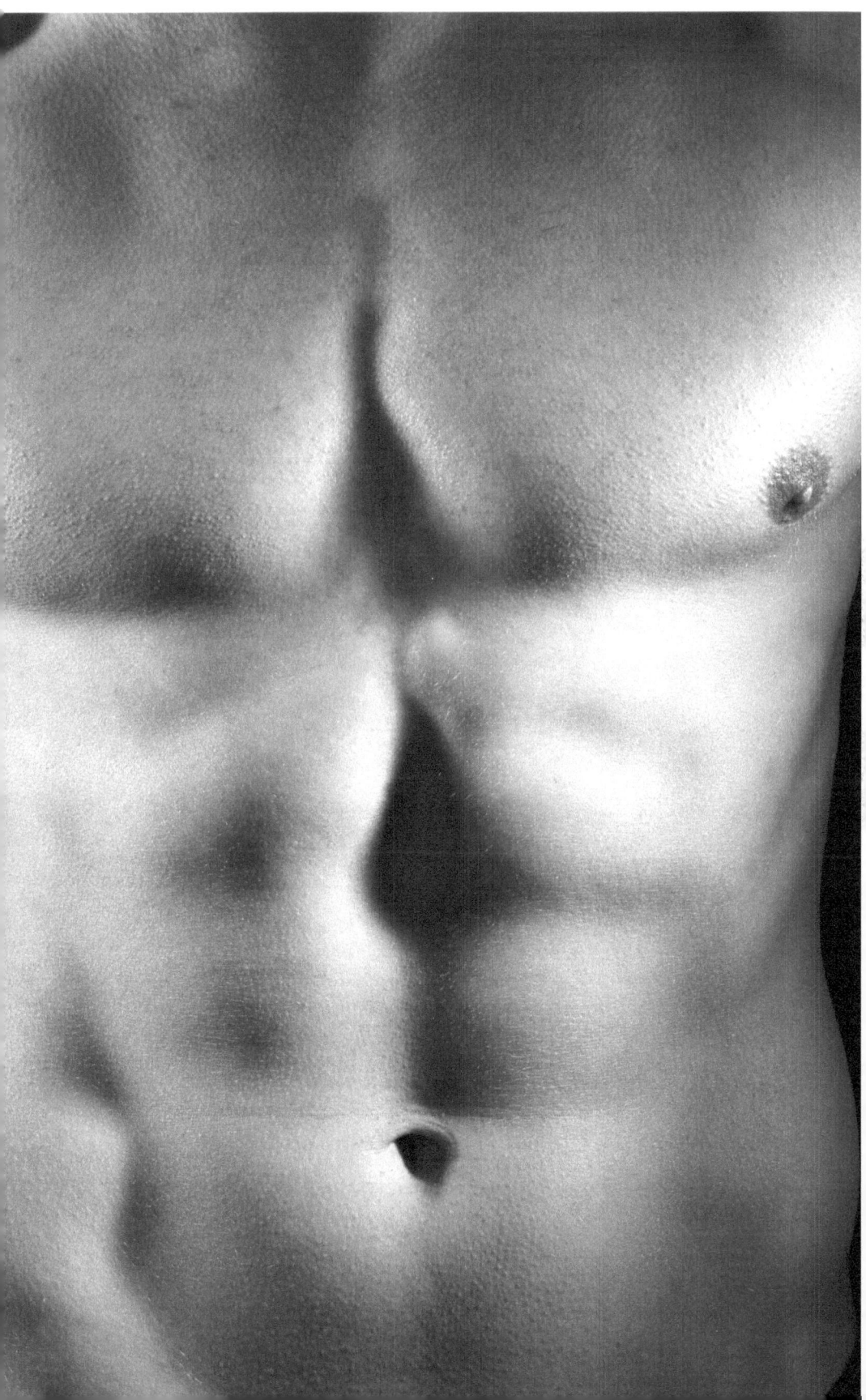

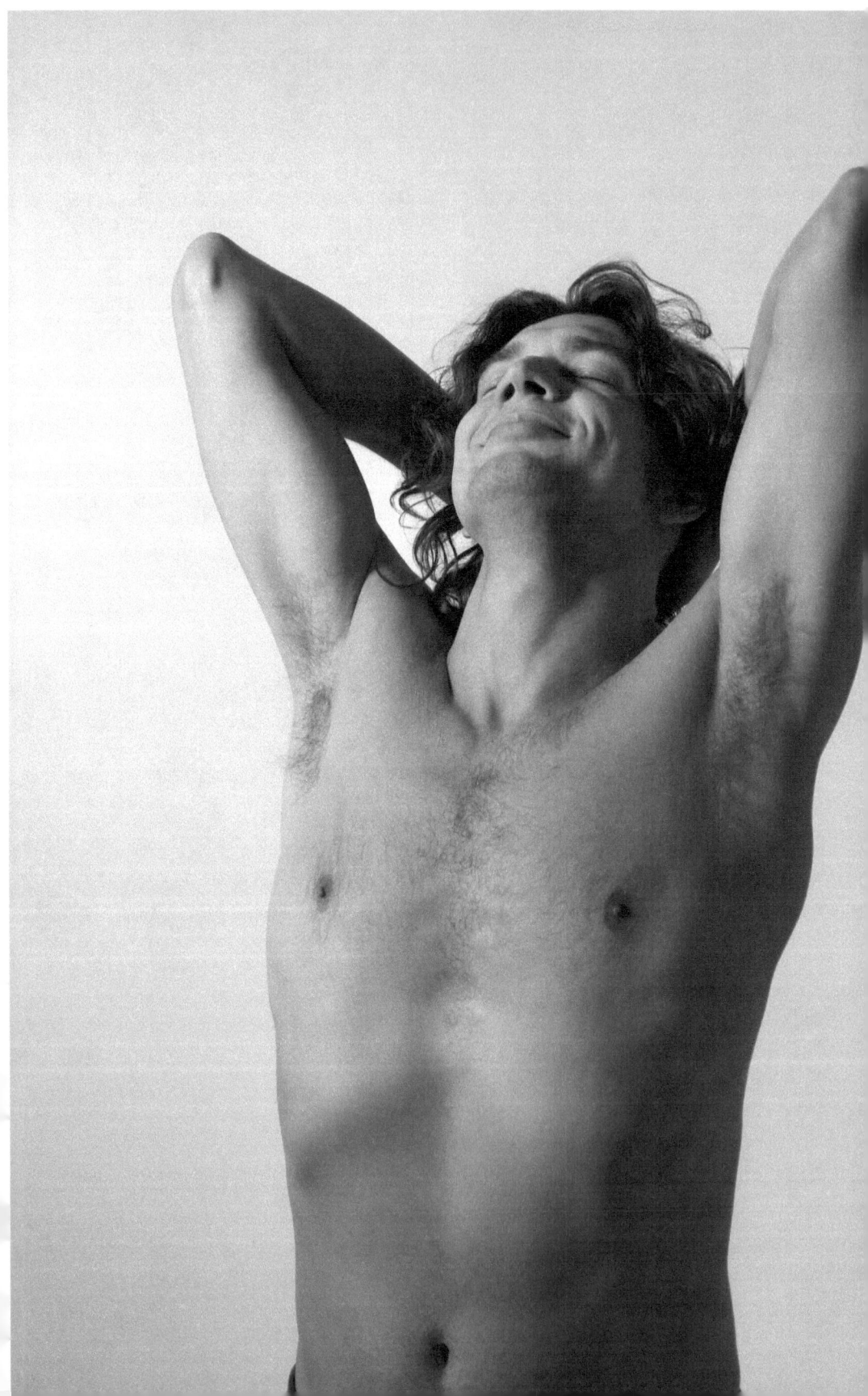

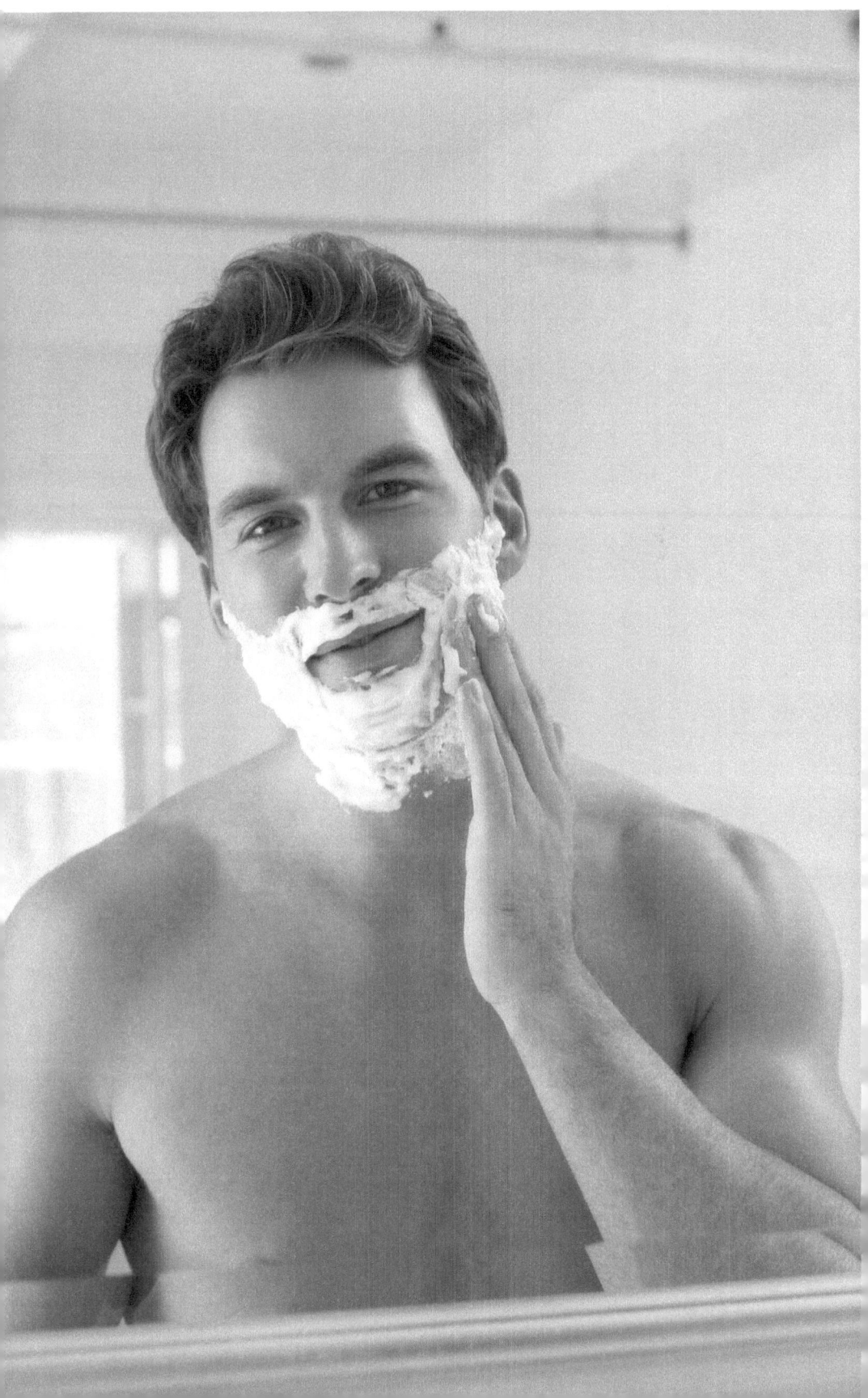

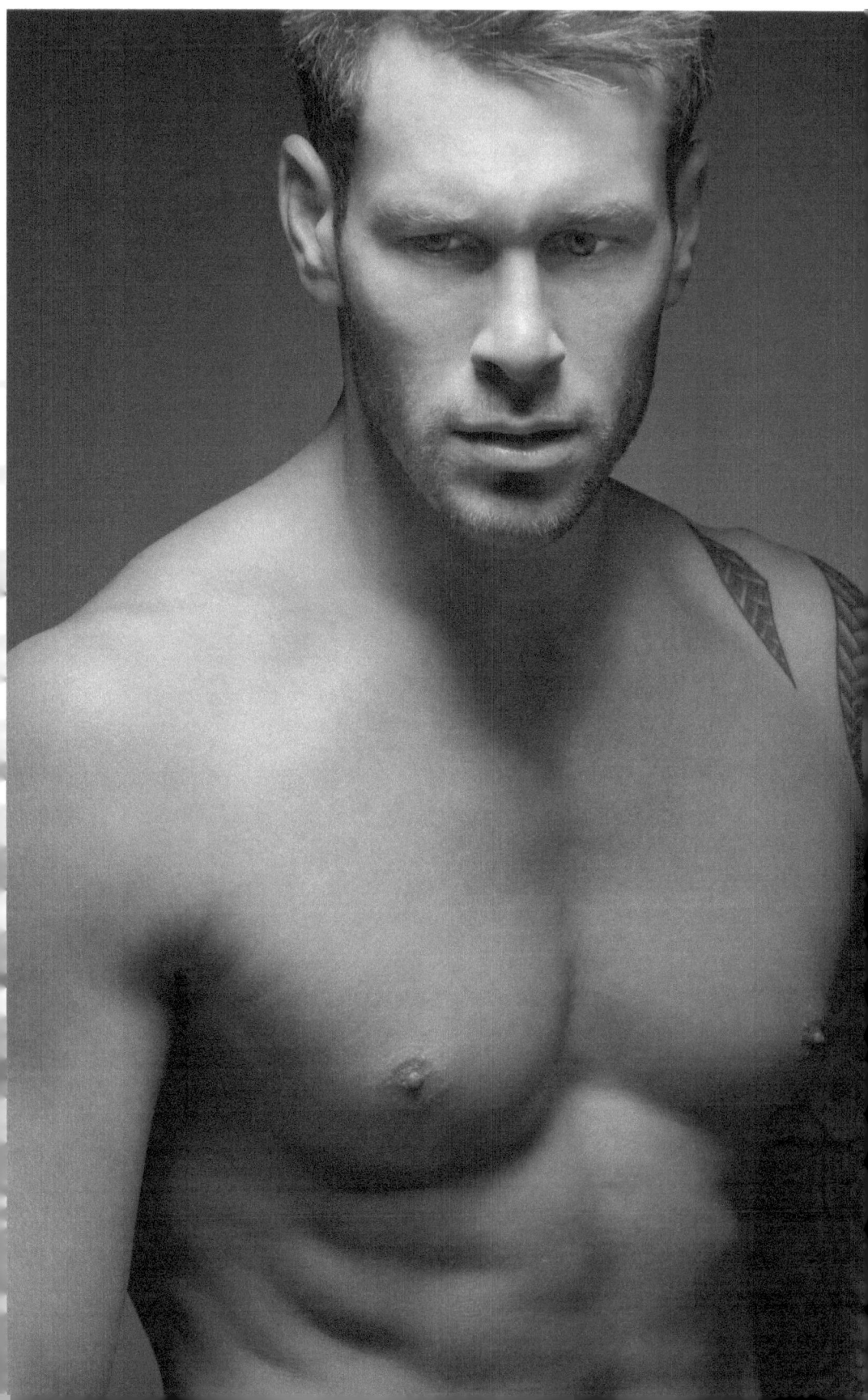

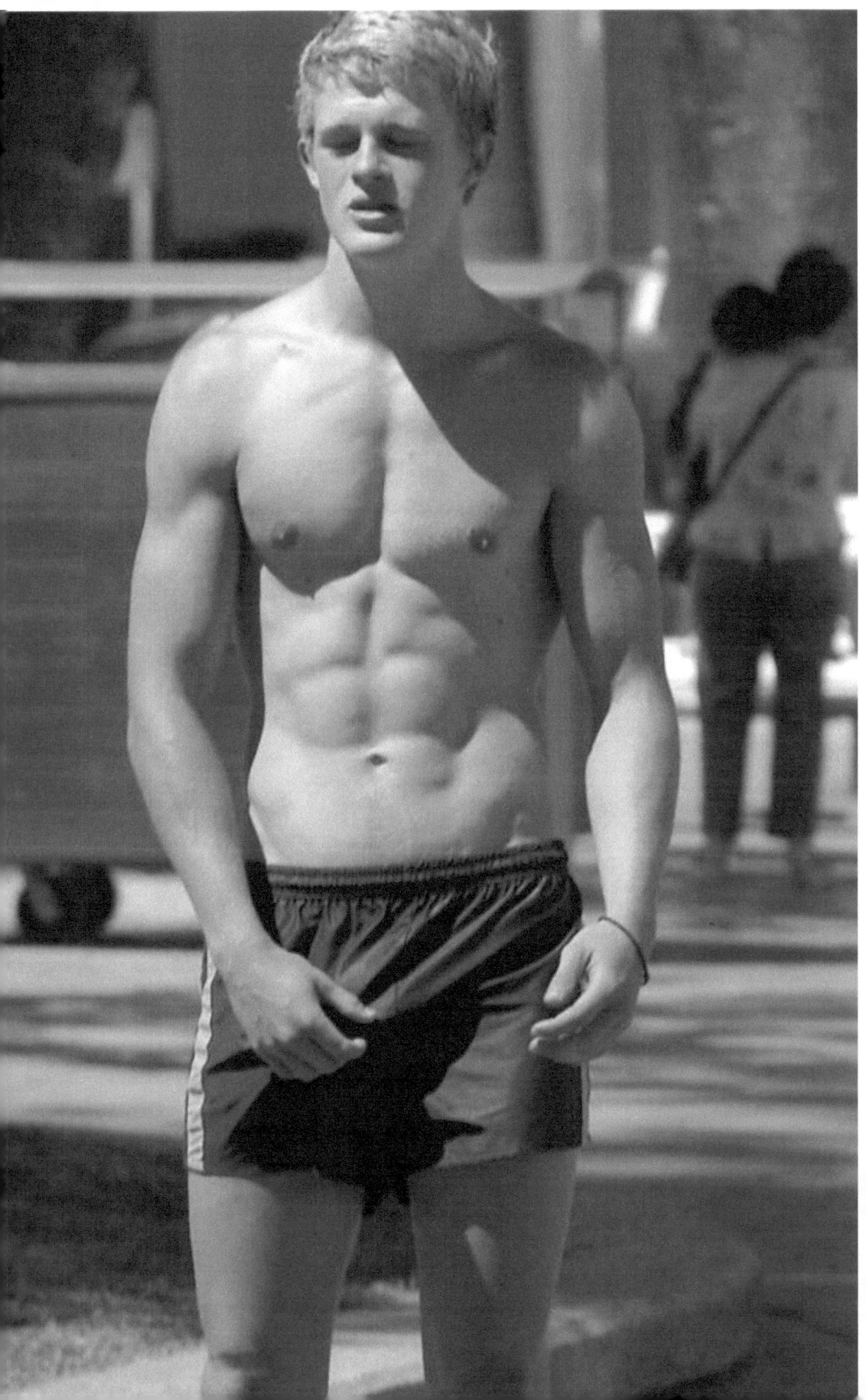

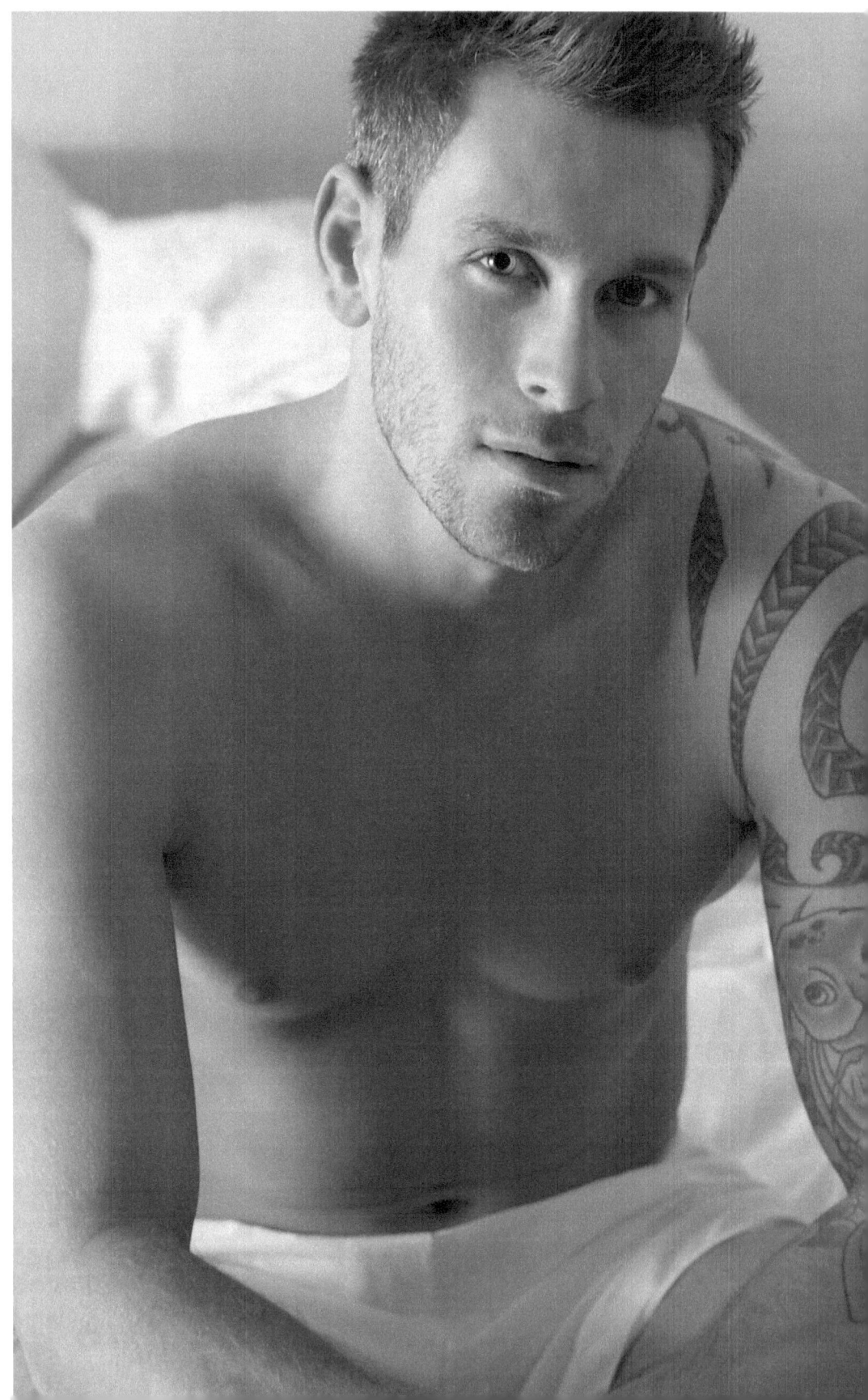

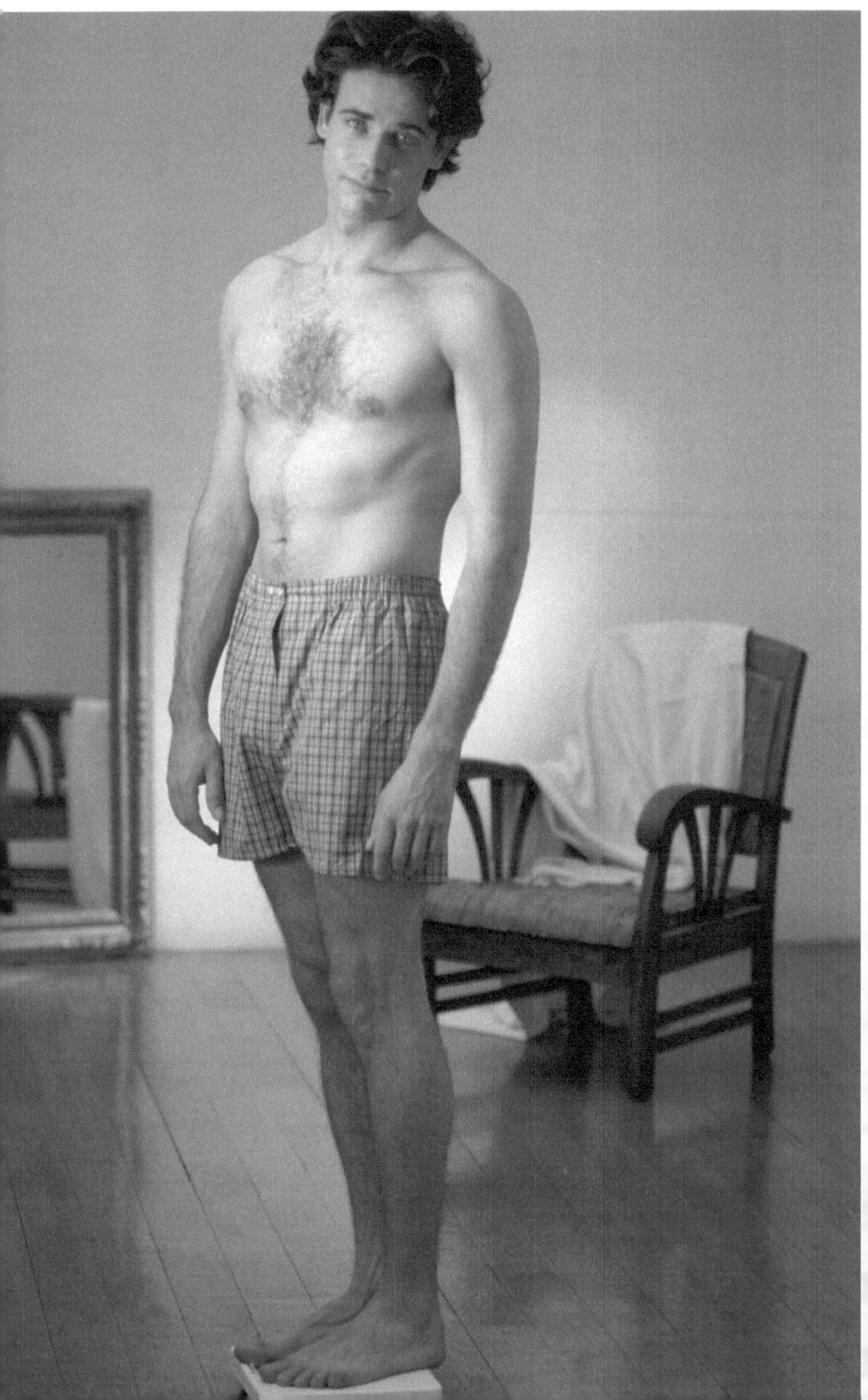

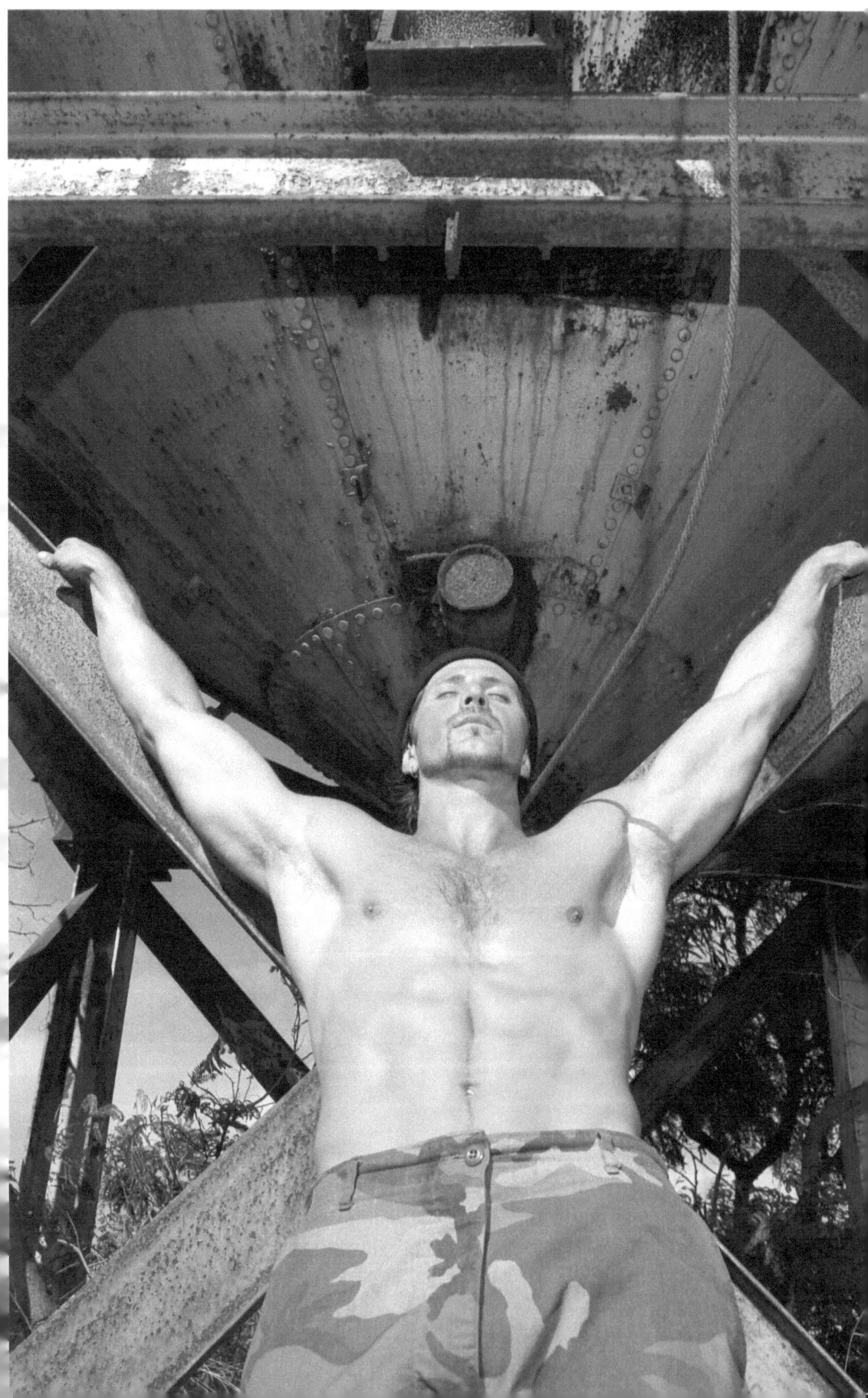

"Did i feel naked being naked?
Yeah. Totally."

Jennifer Lawrence

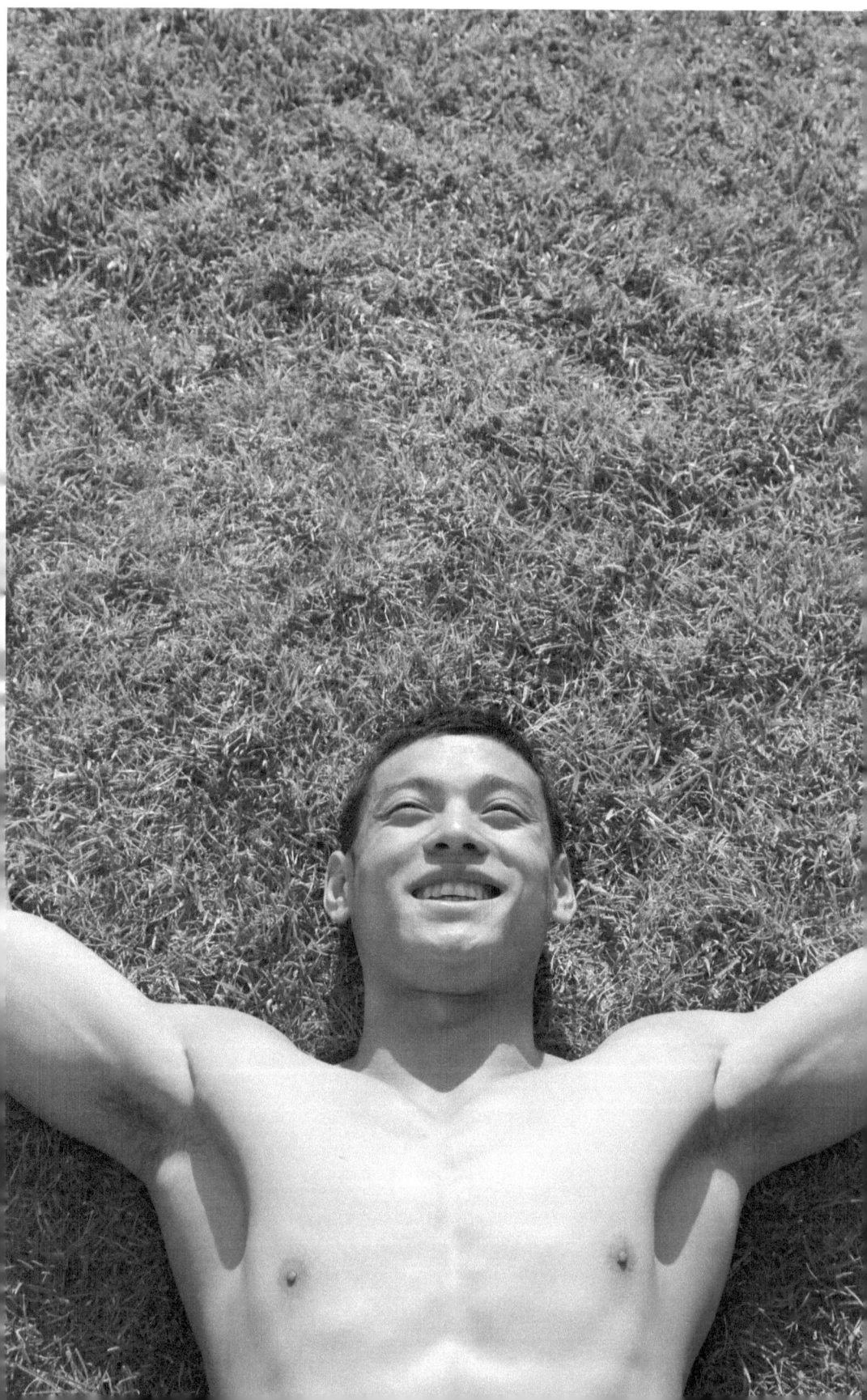

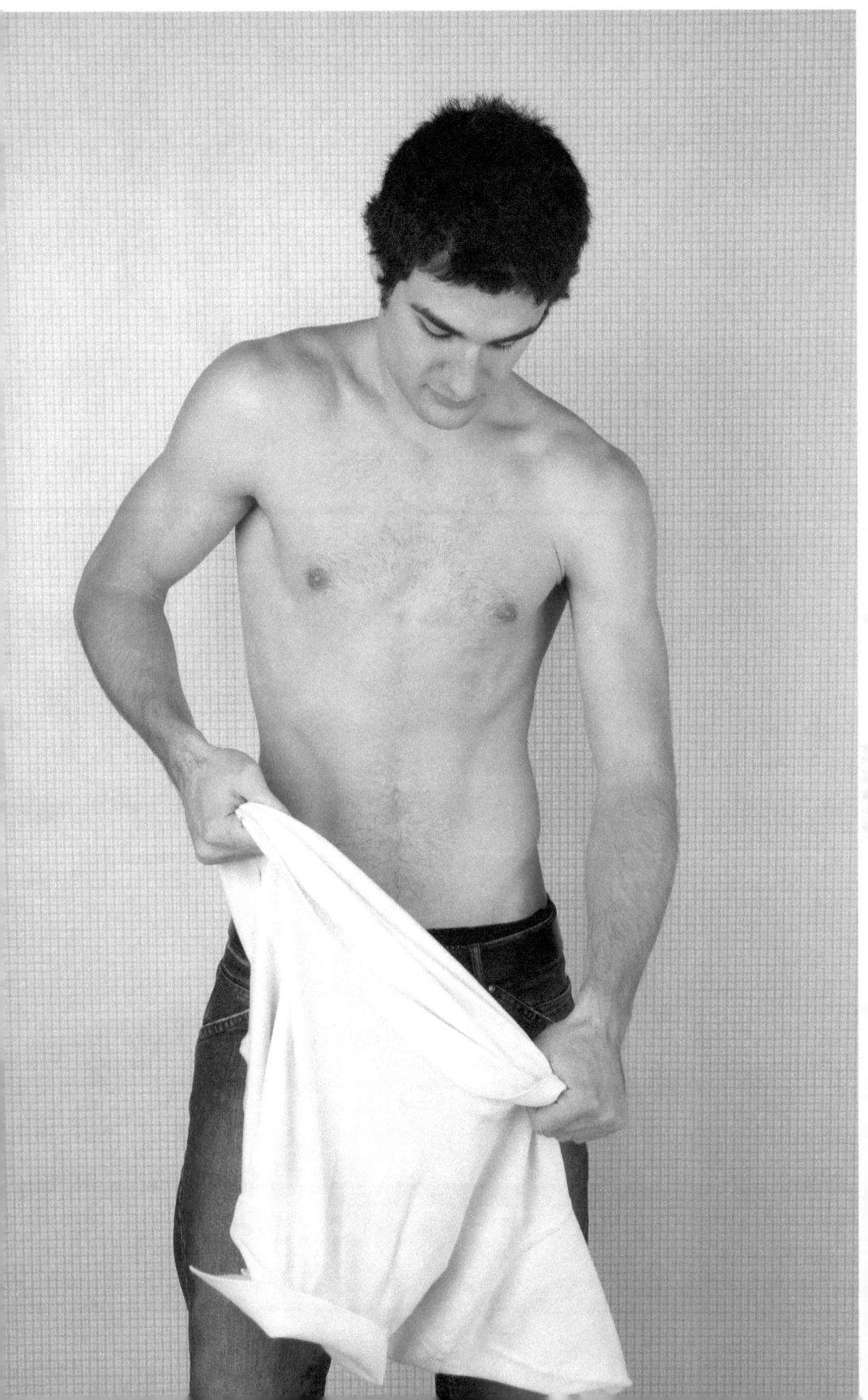

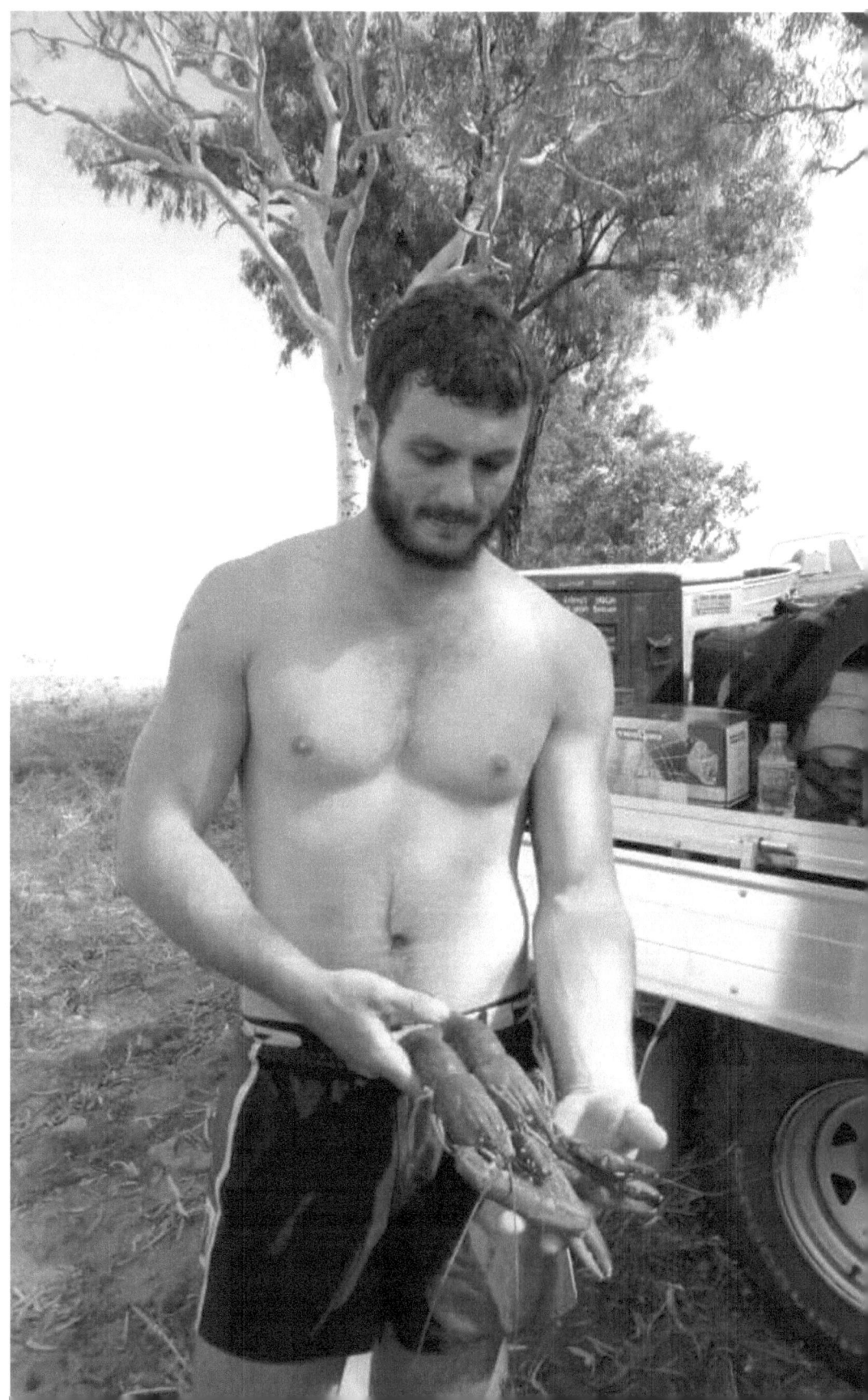

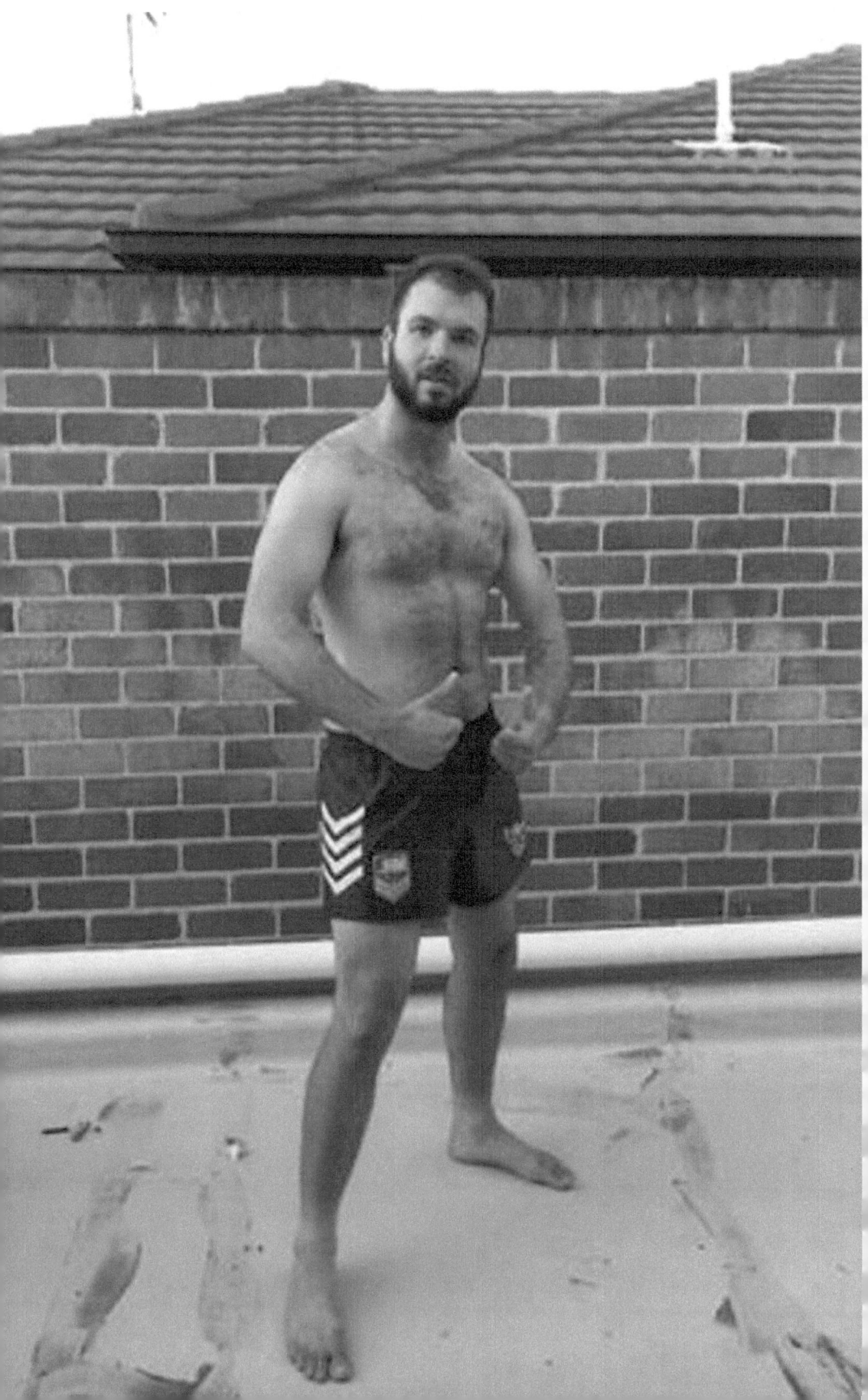

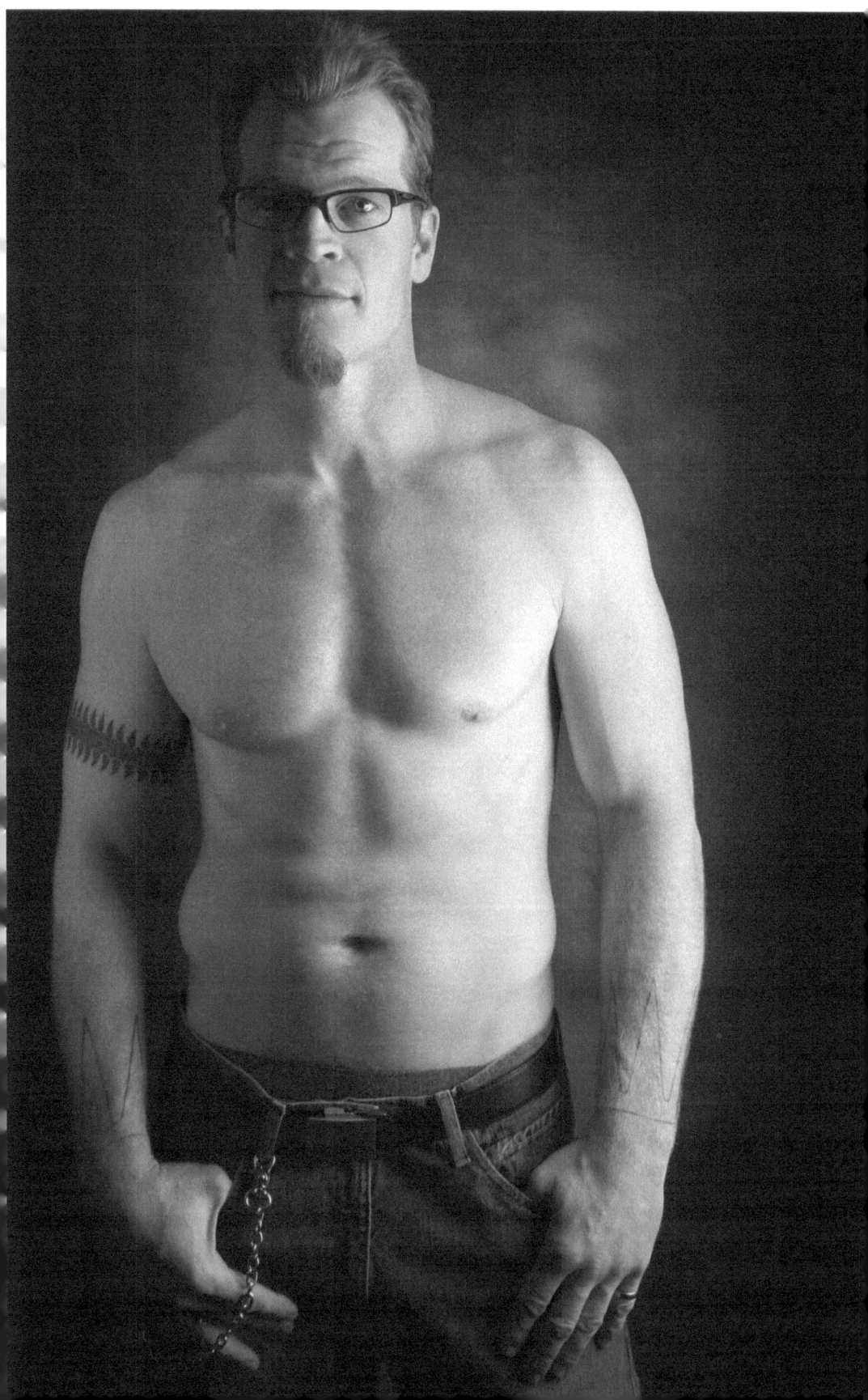

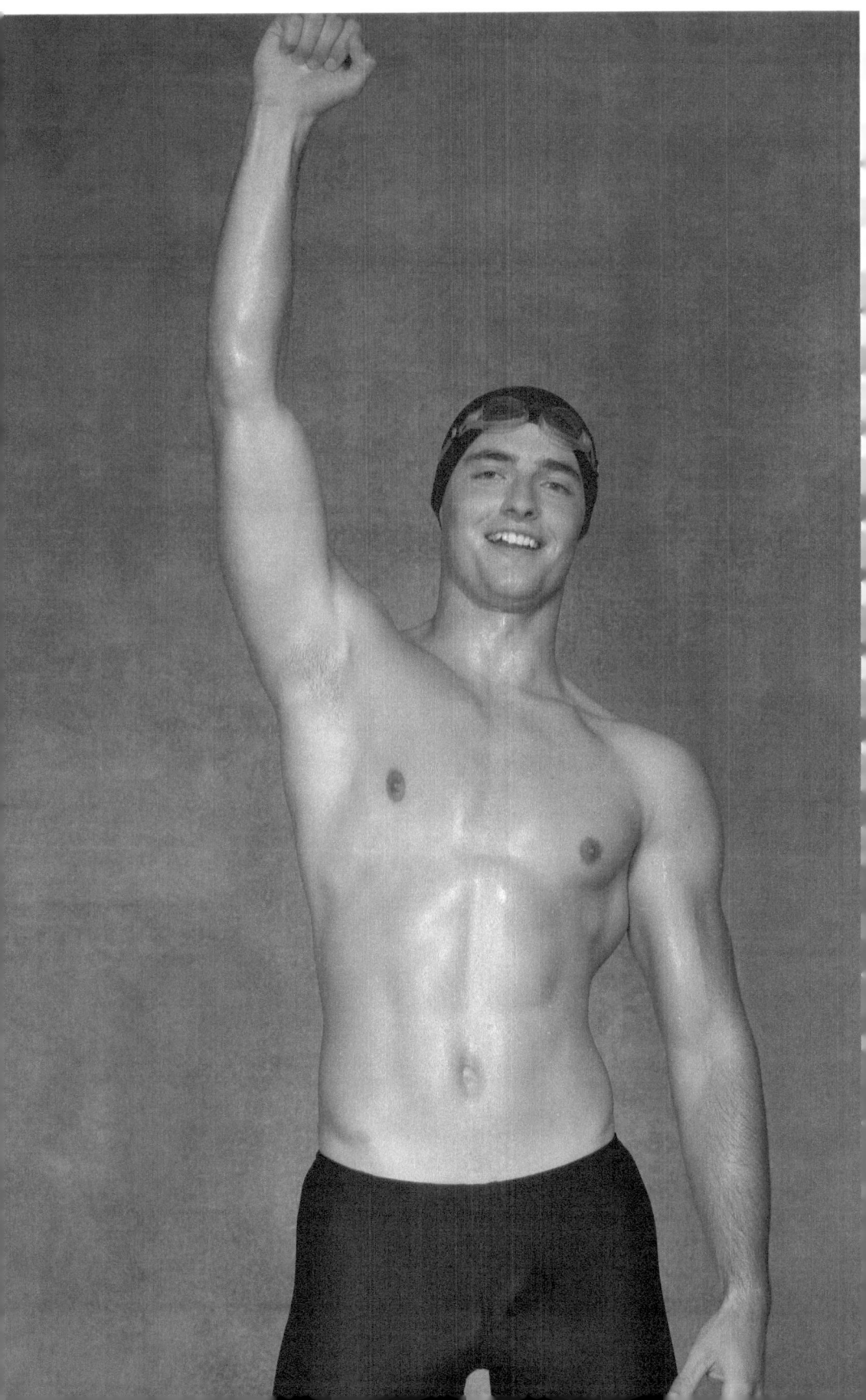

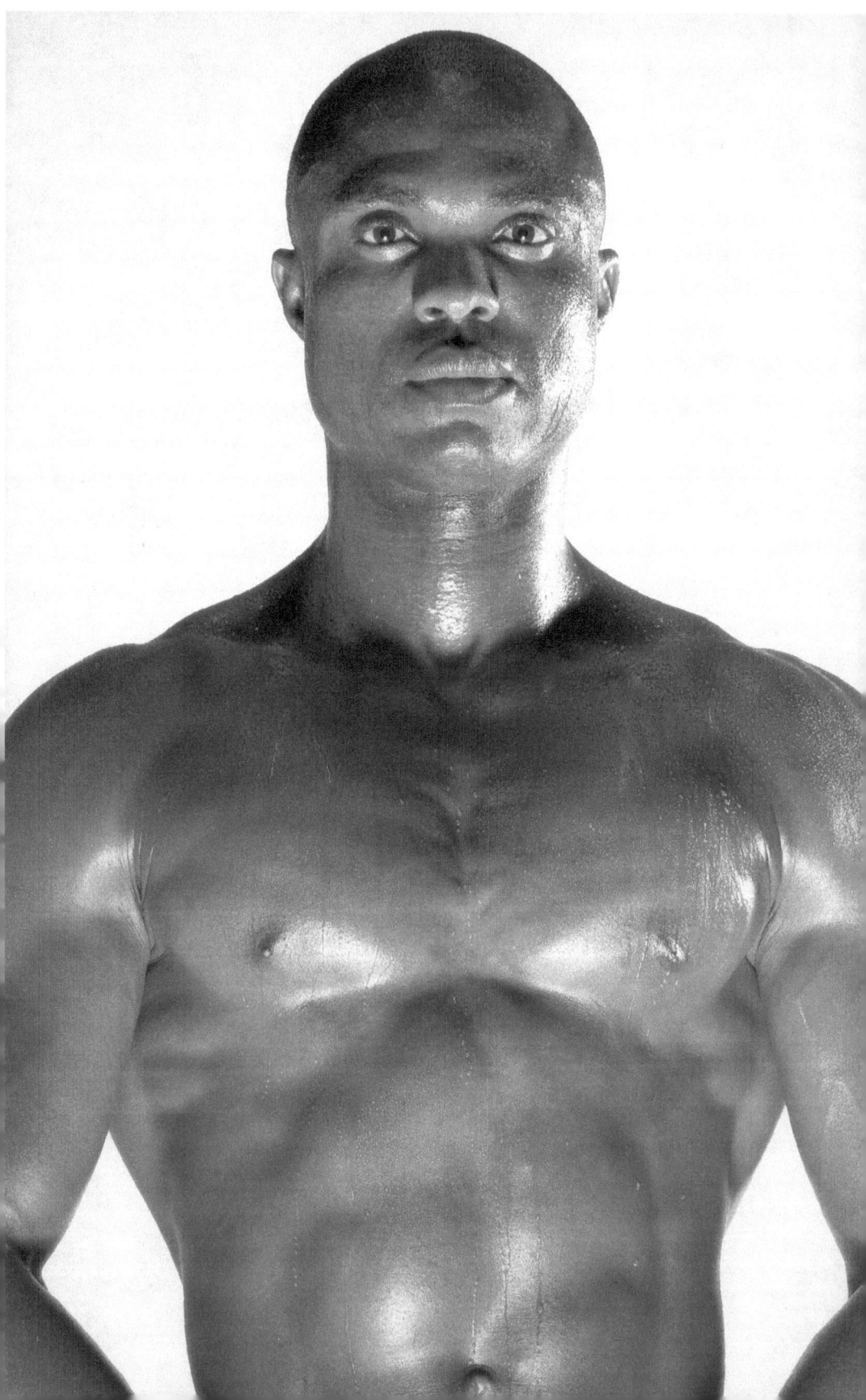

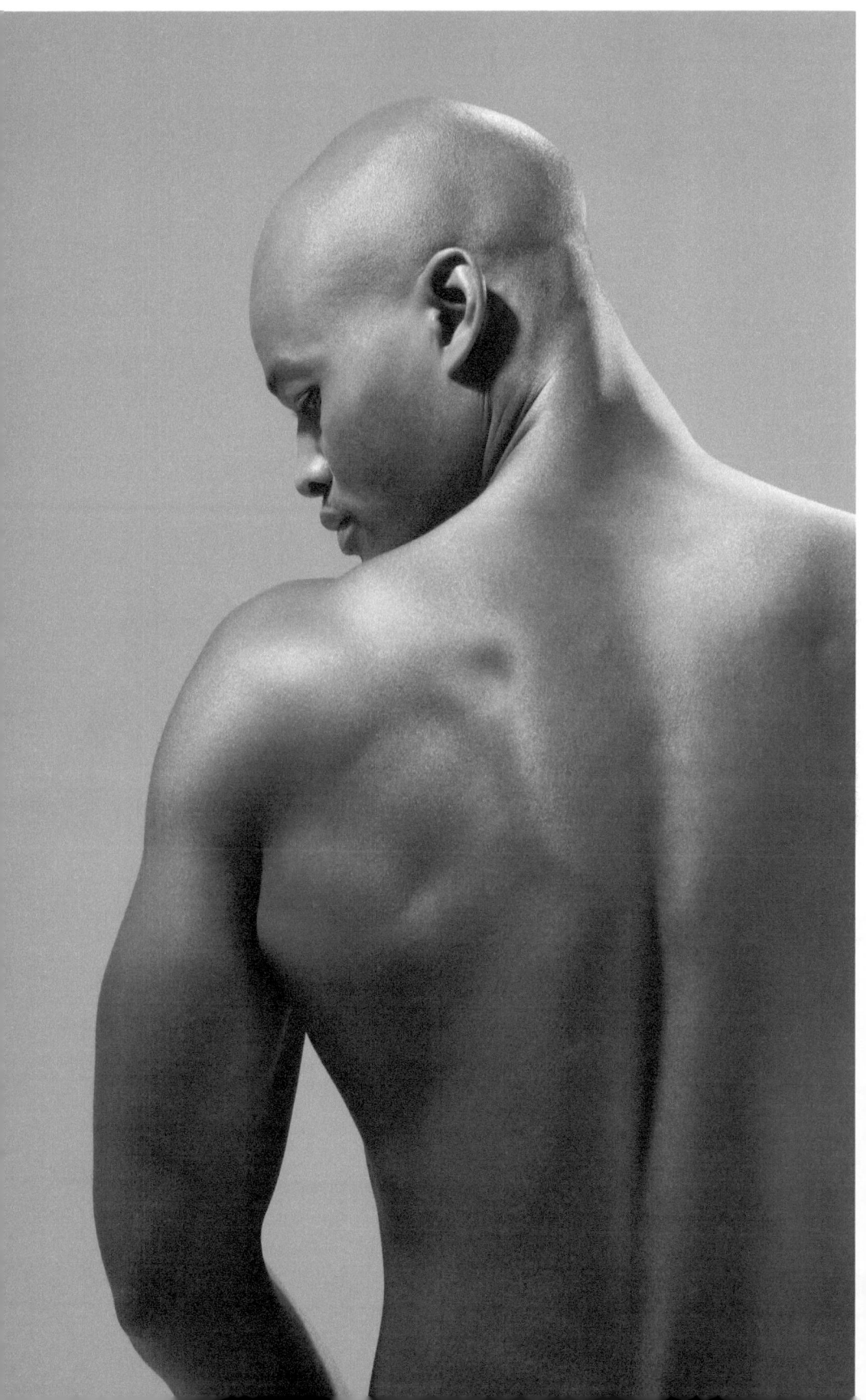

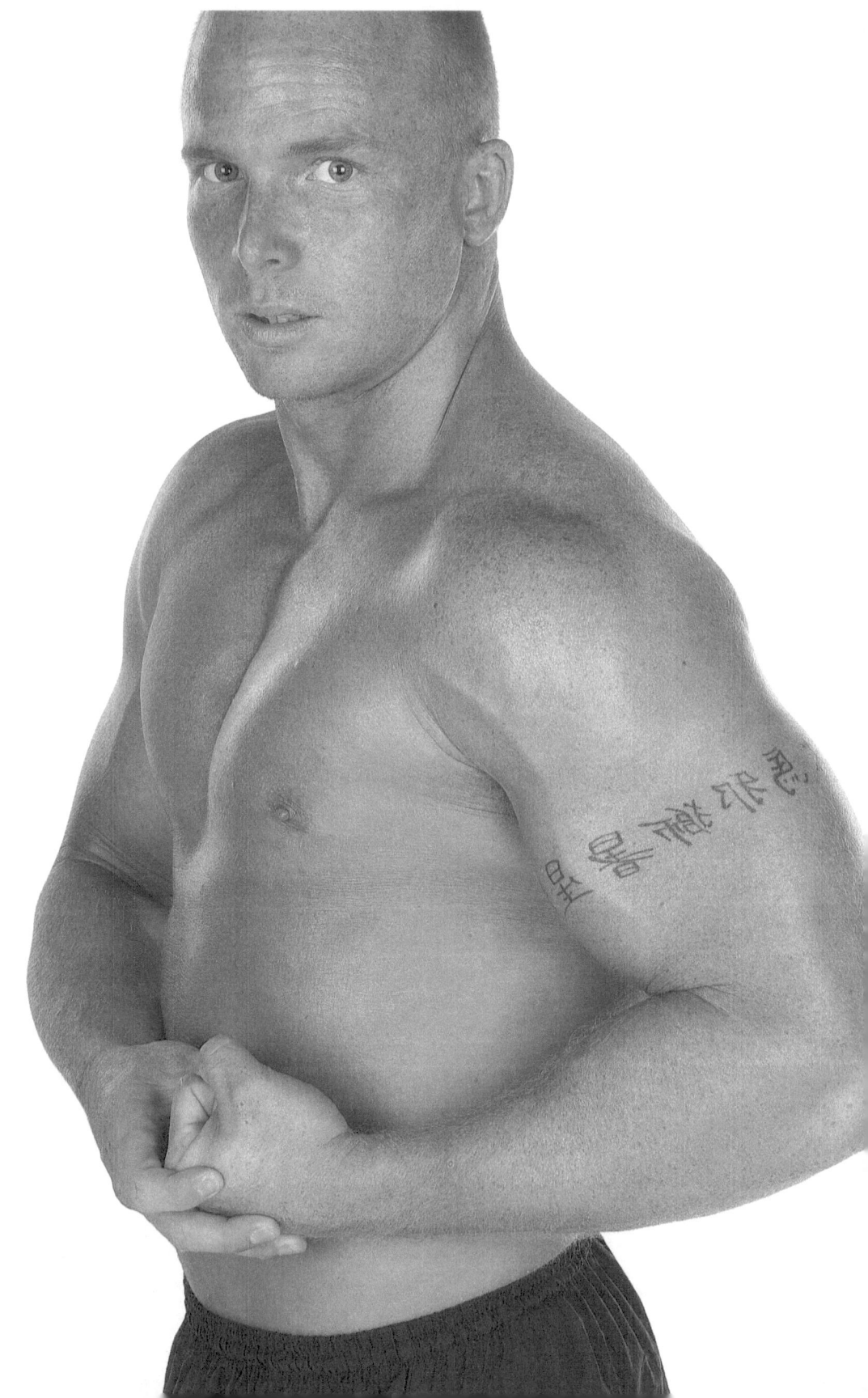

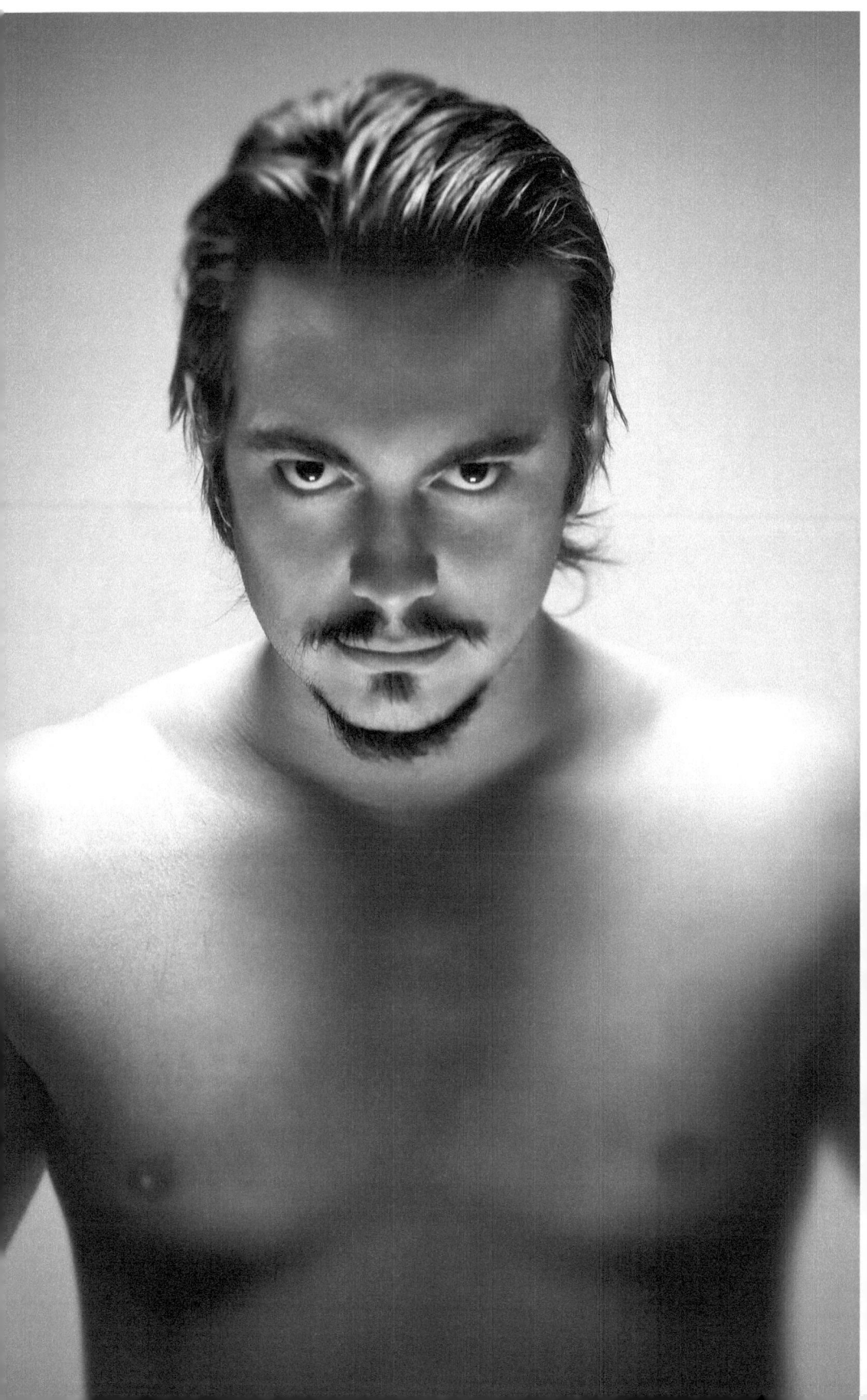

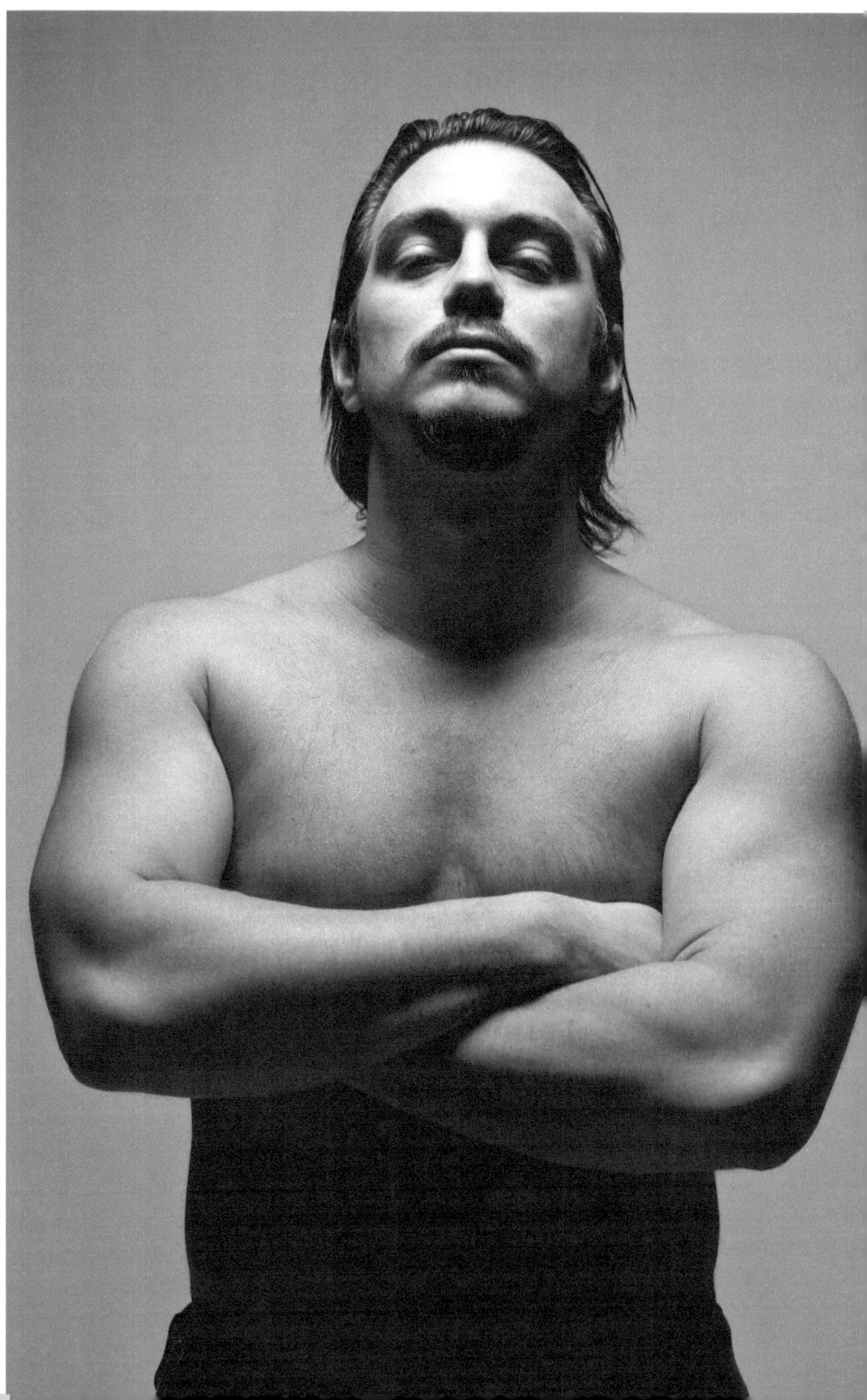

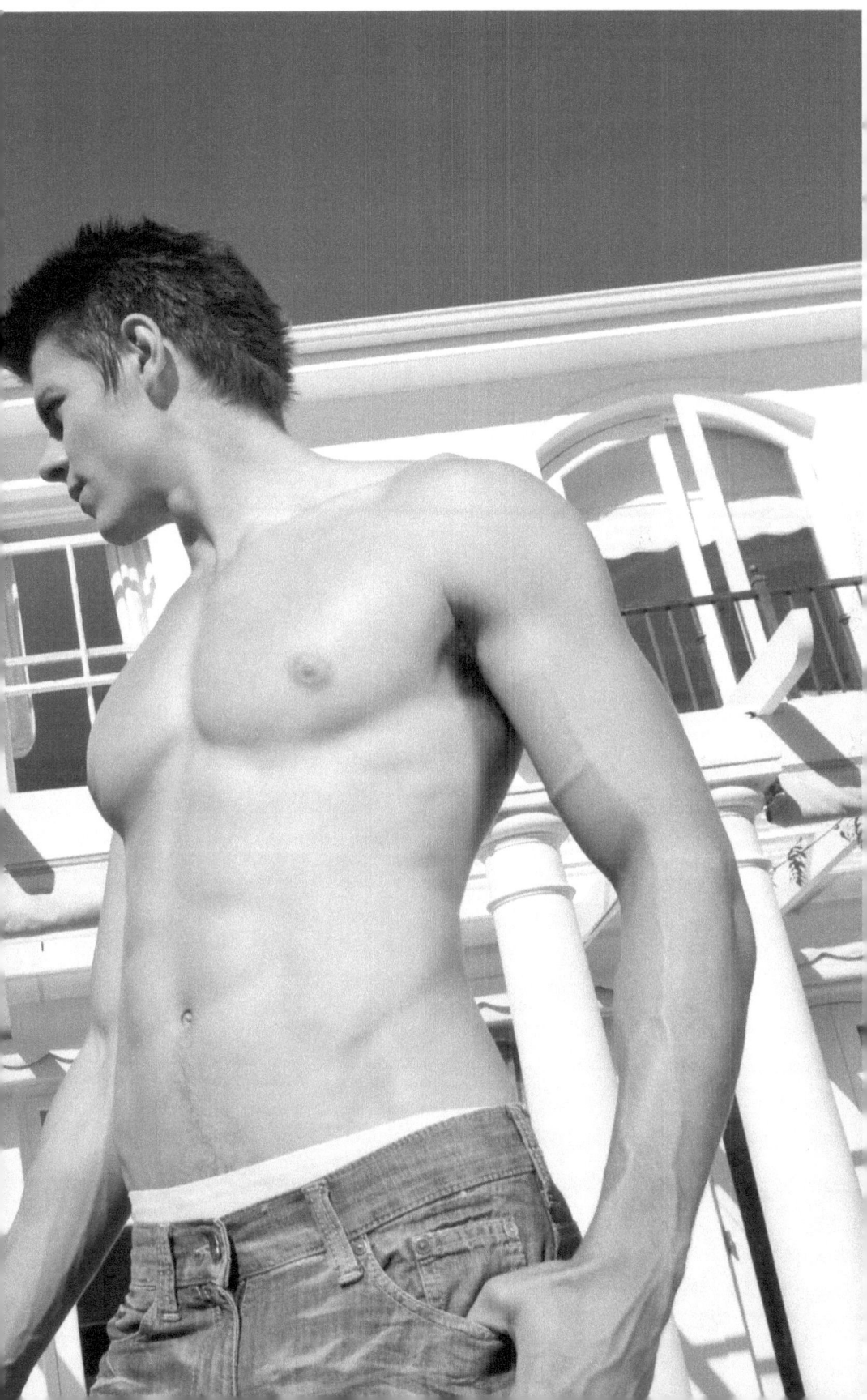

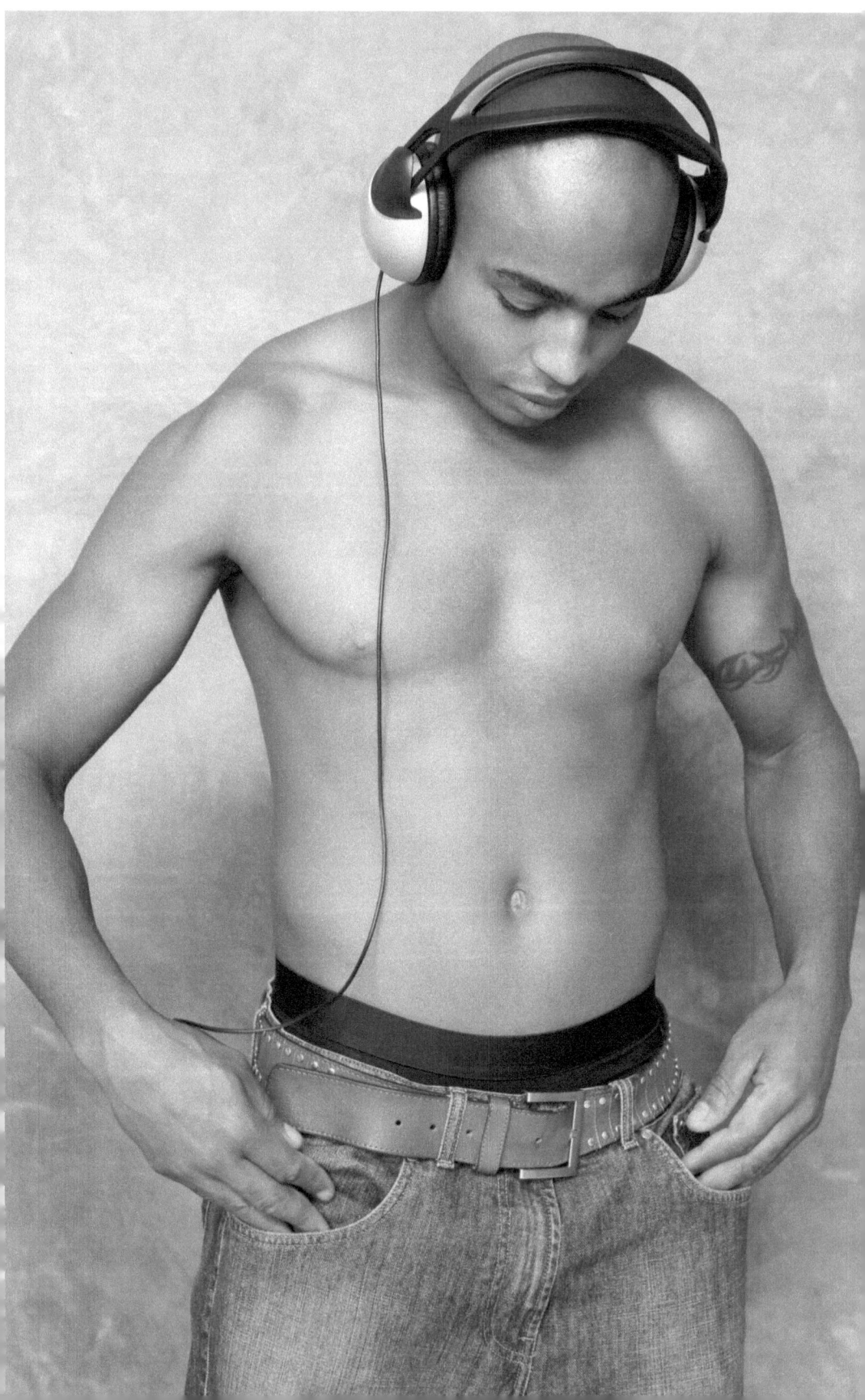

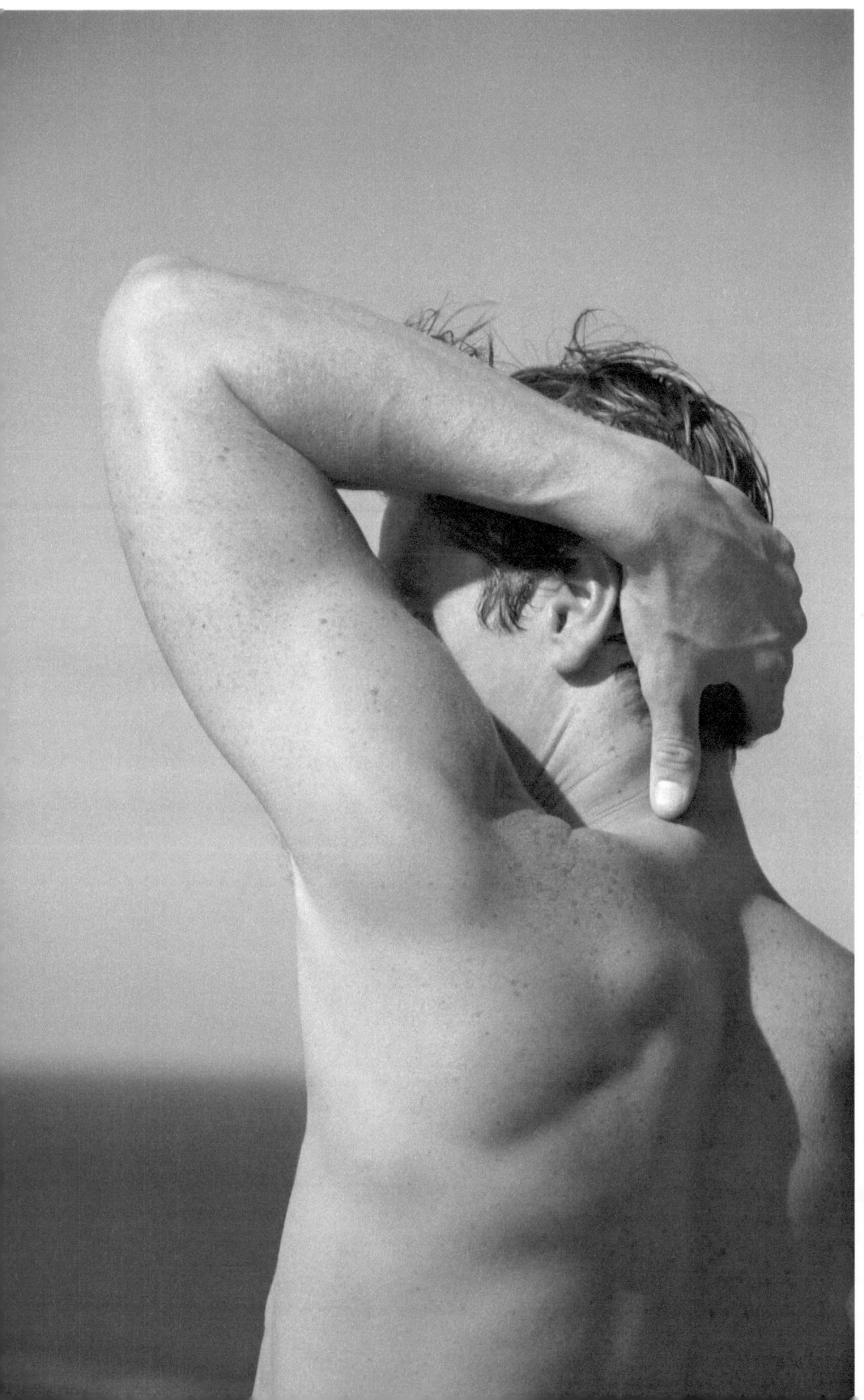

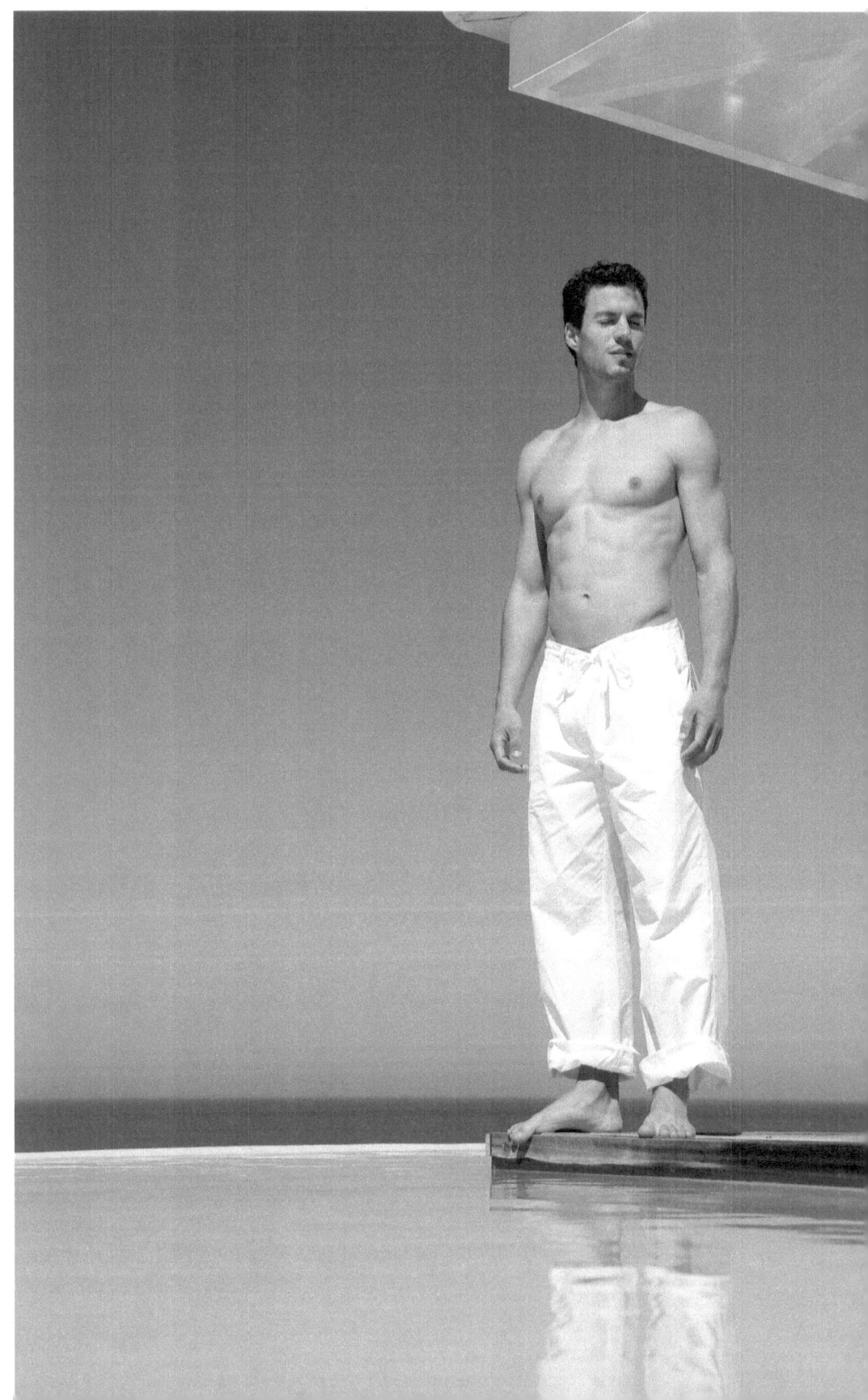

"Shoes and clothing damage our ability to survive naked in the wilderness."

Steve Mann

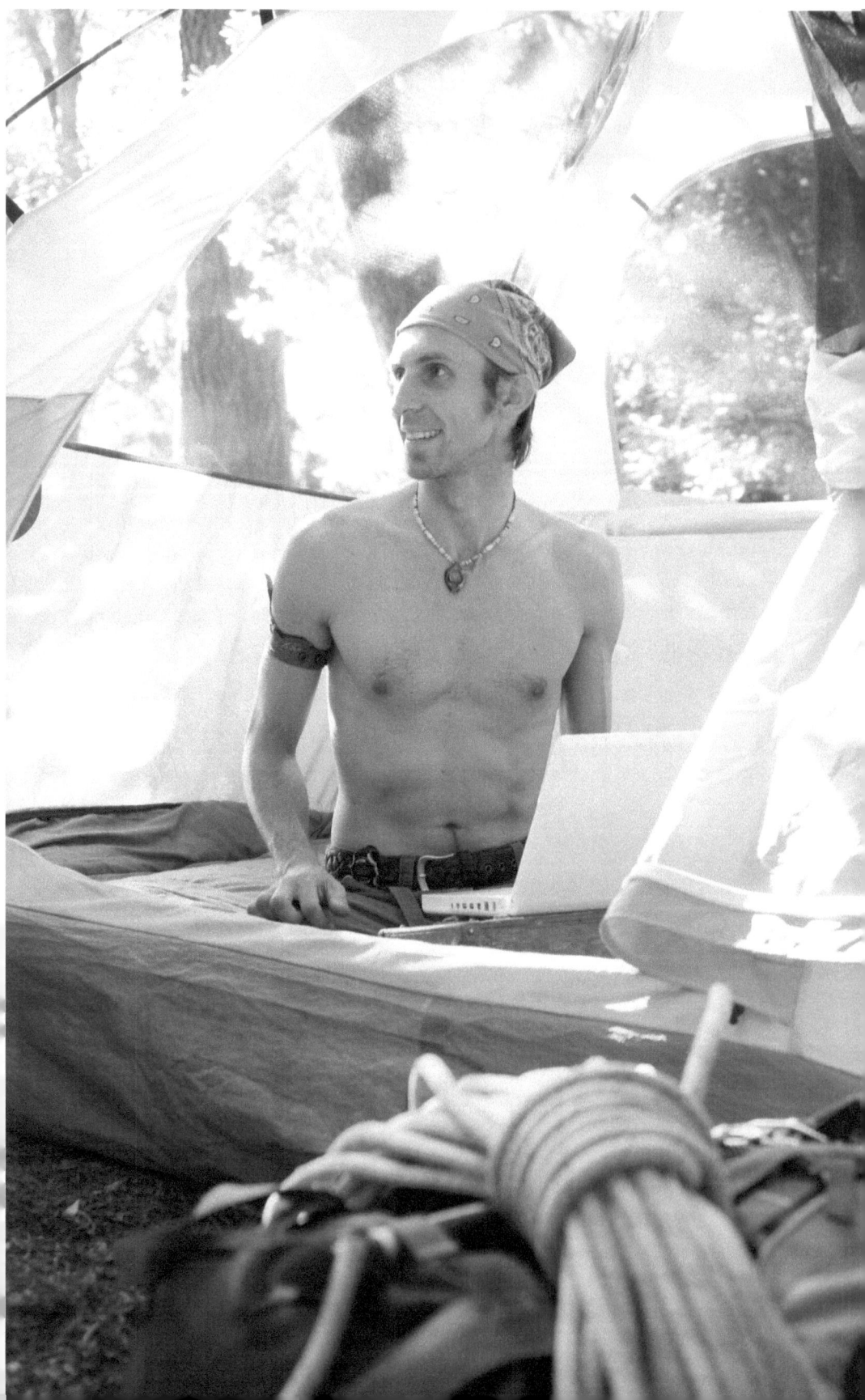

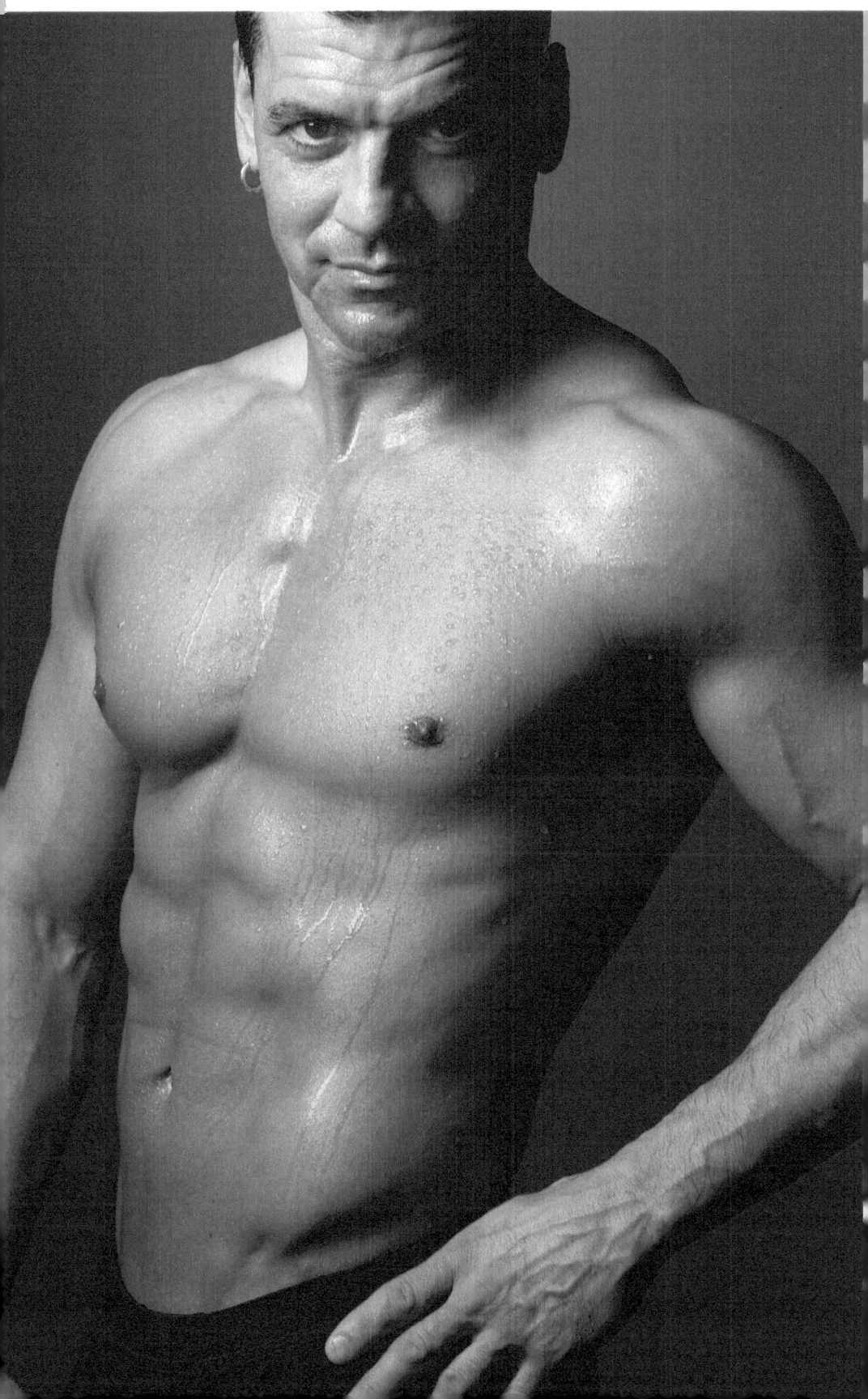

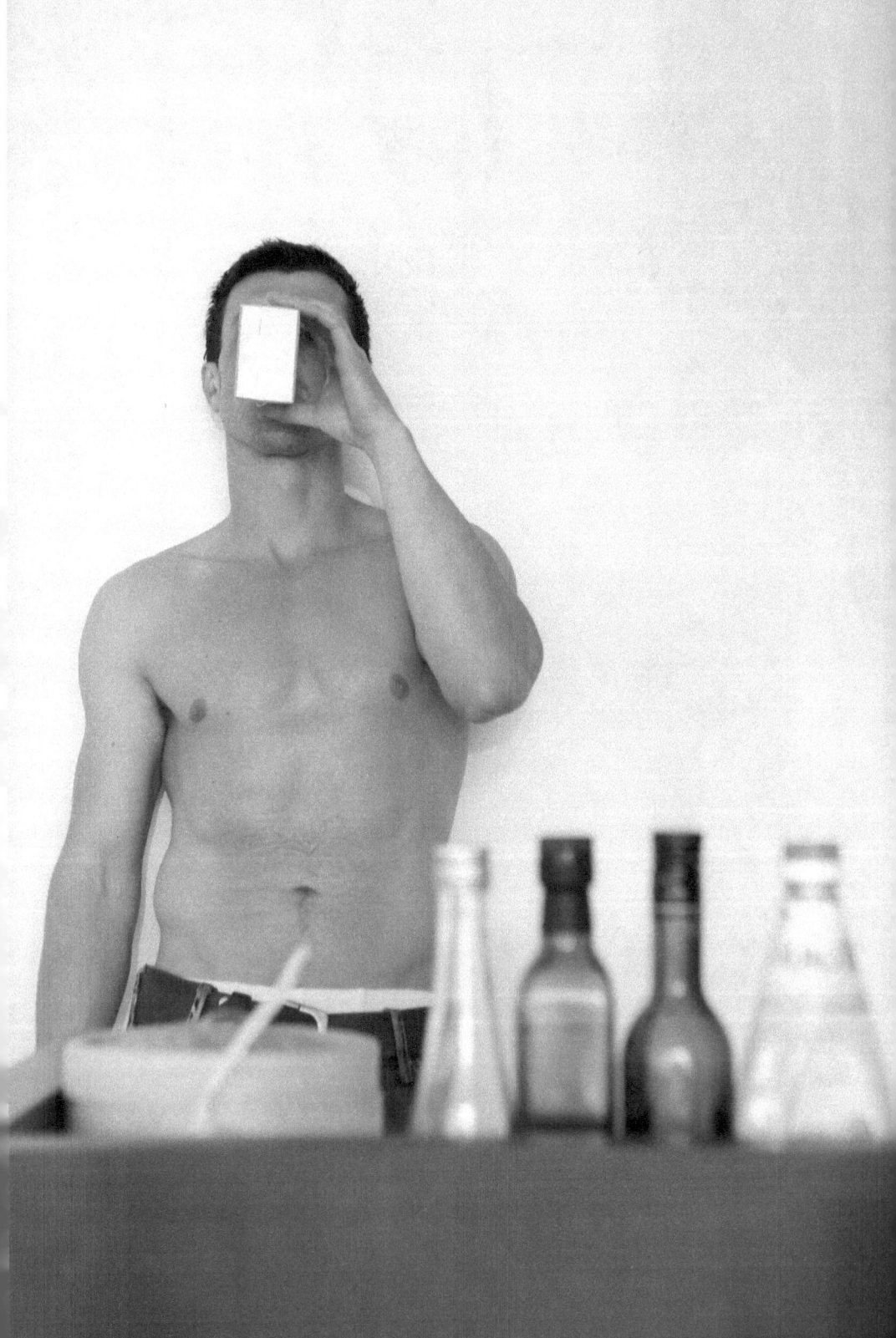

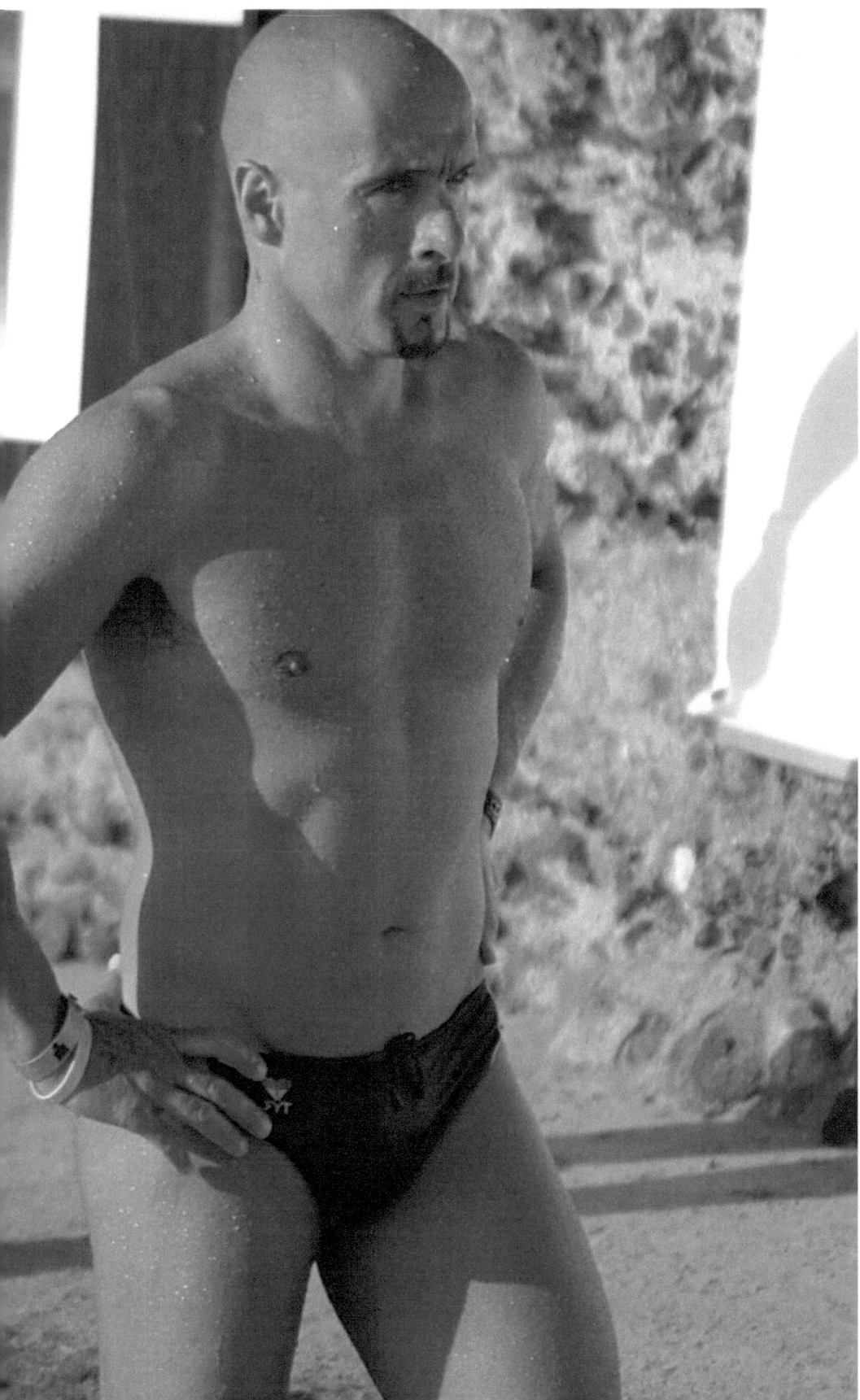

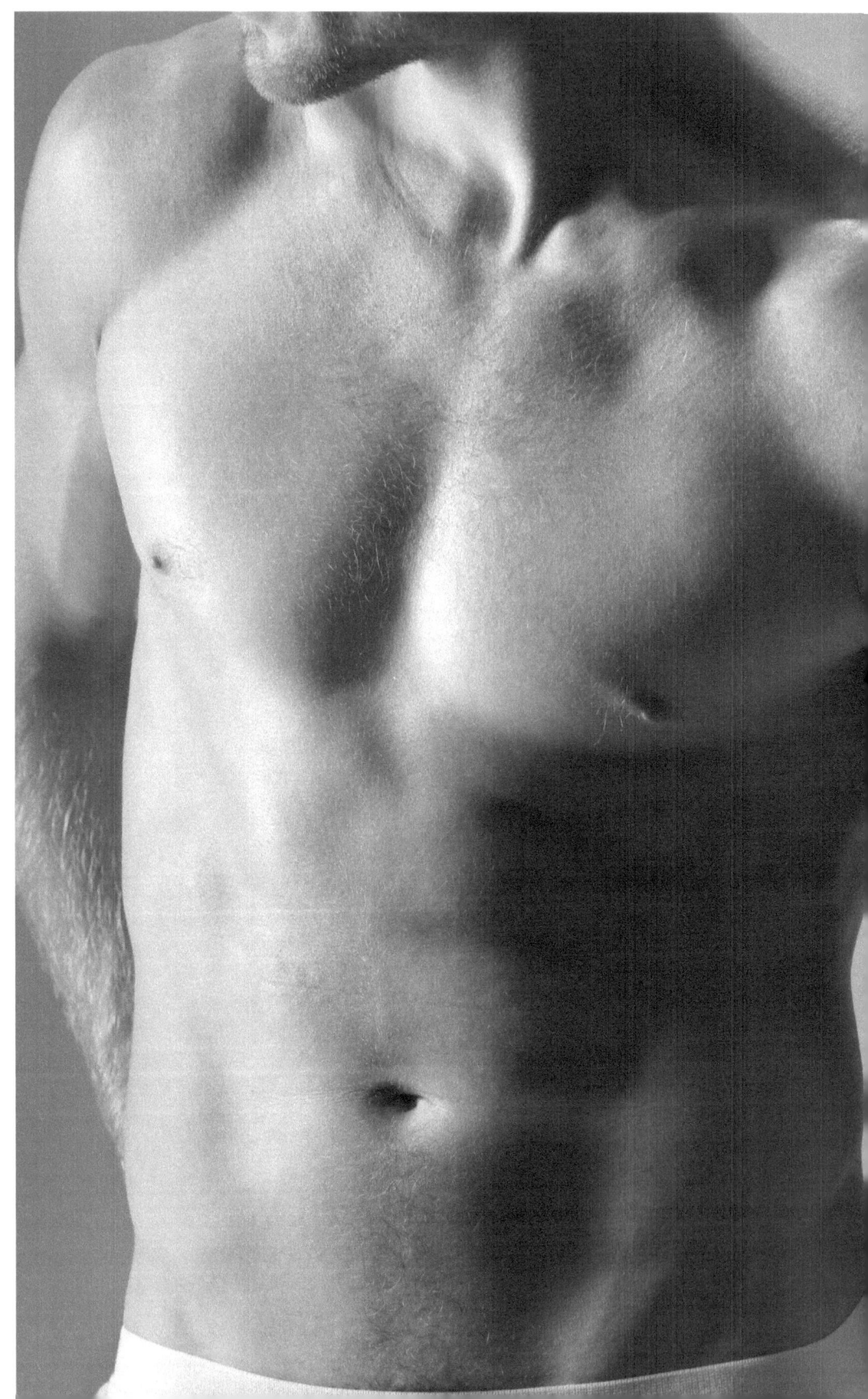

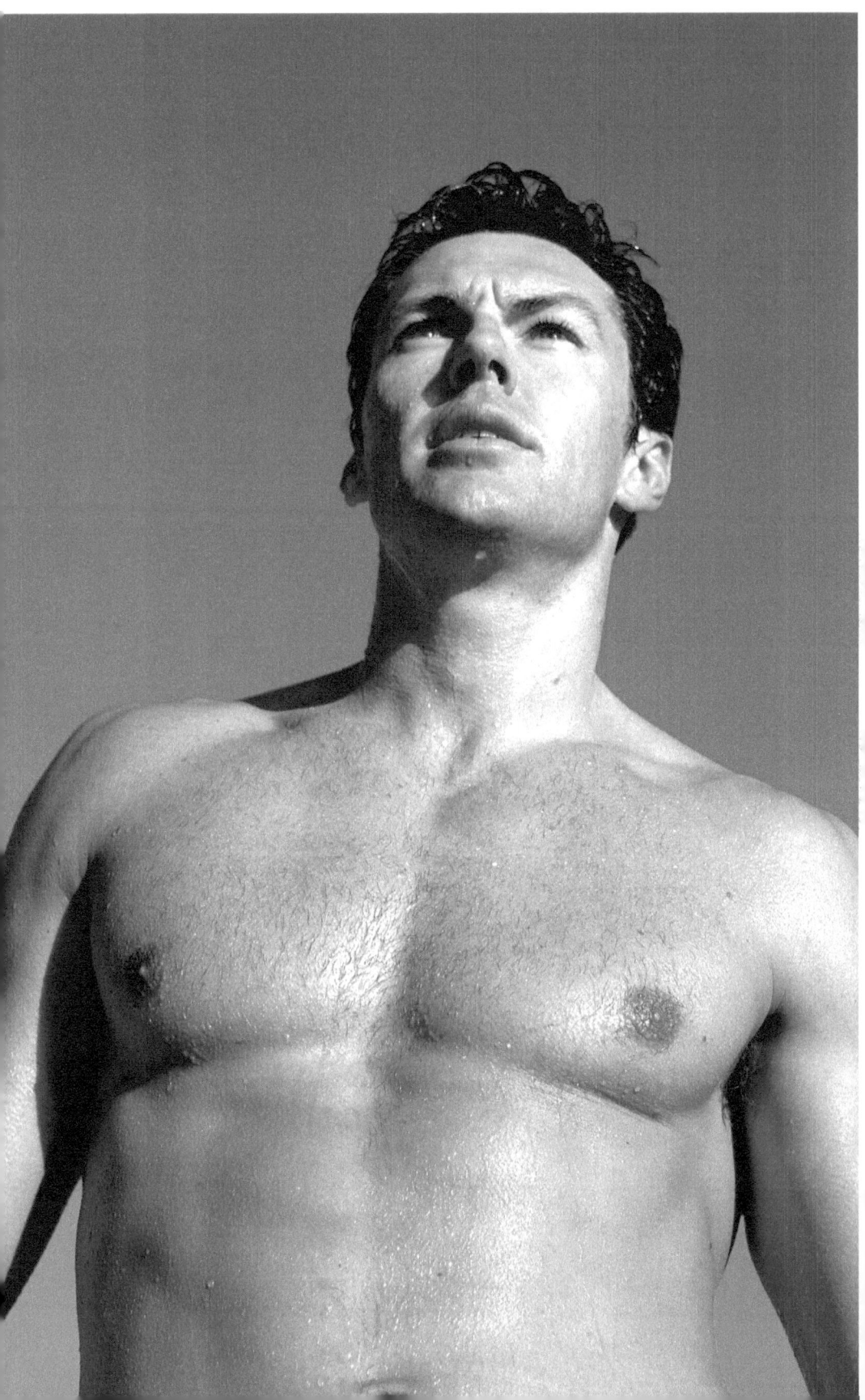

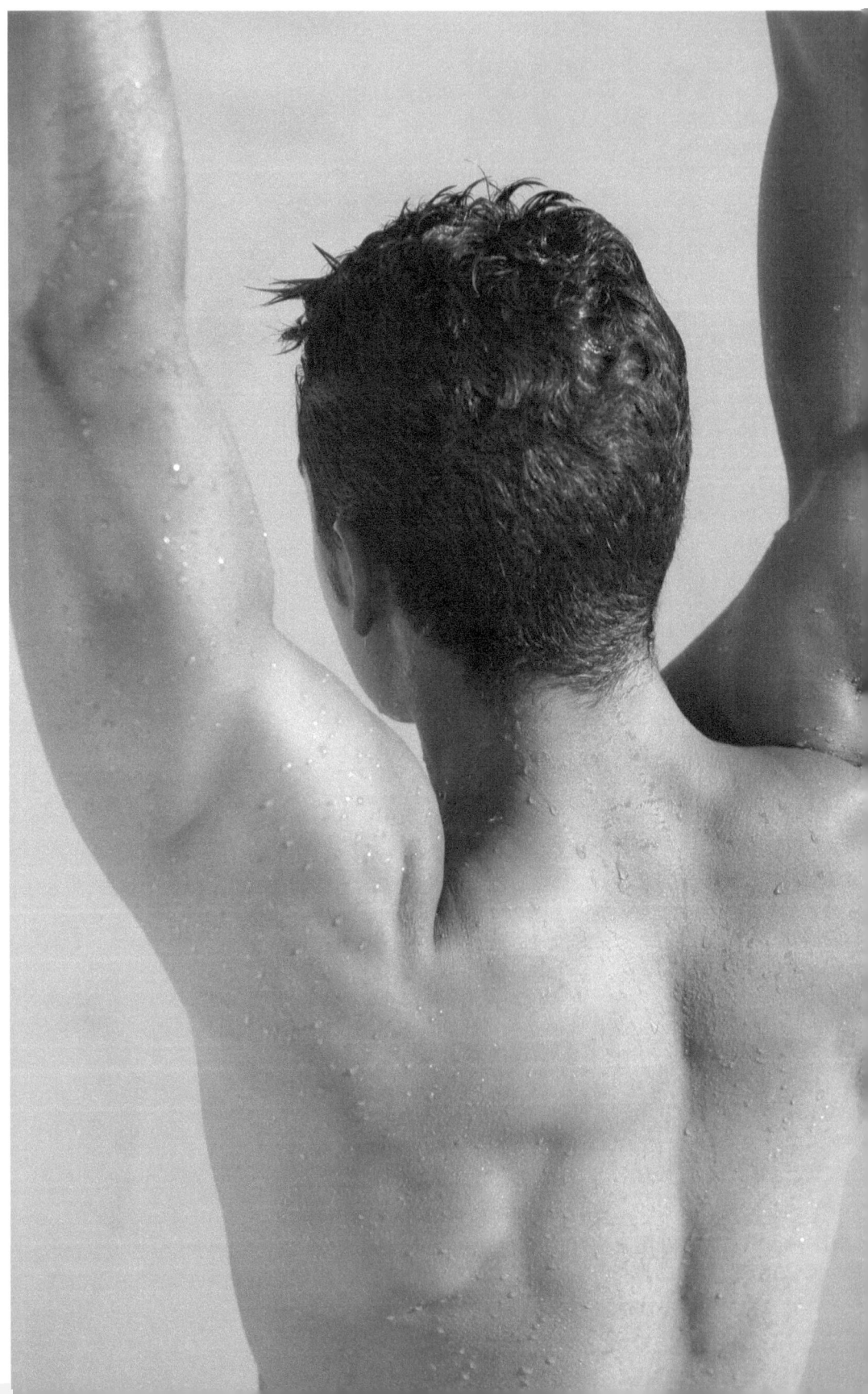

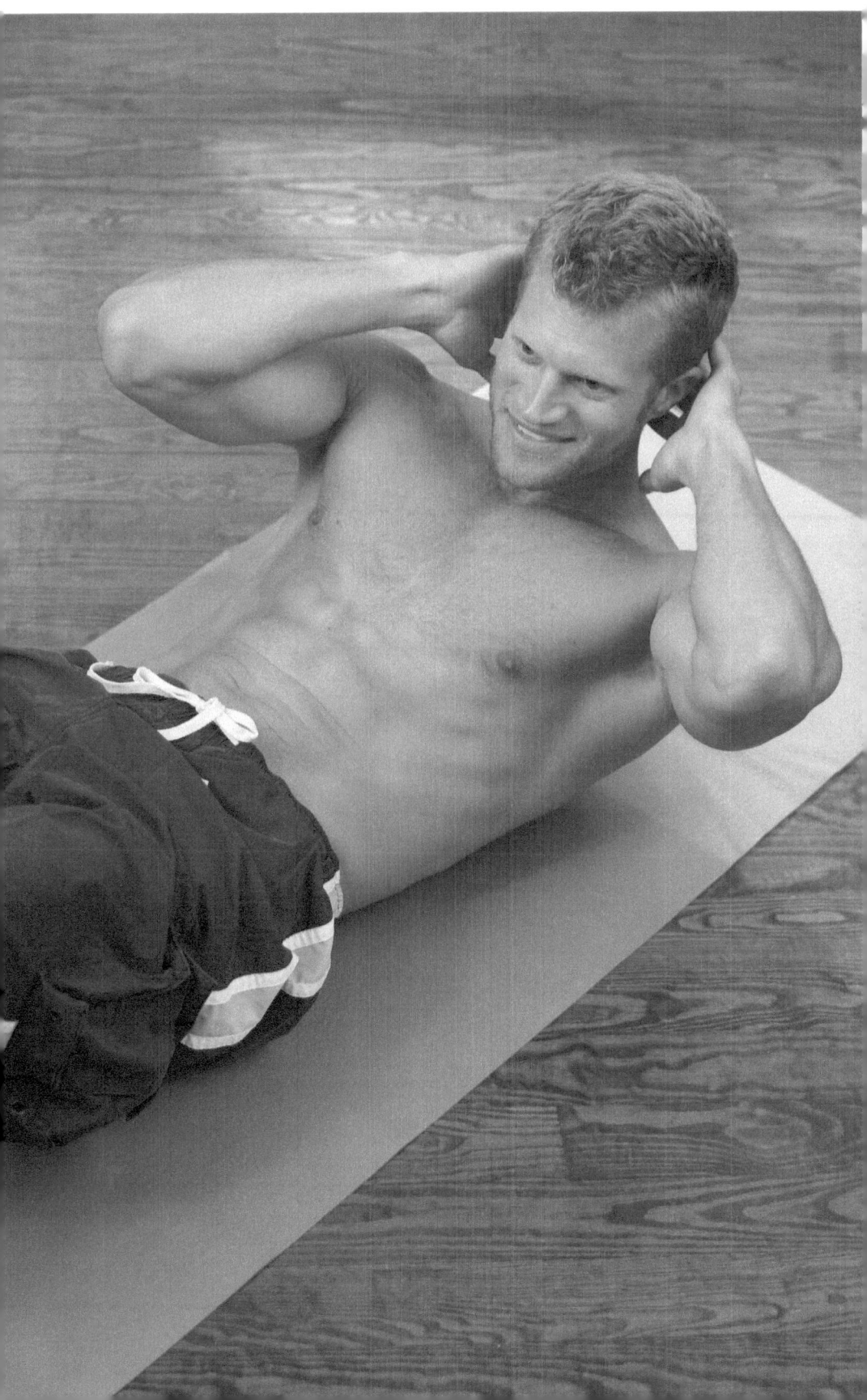

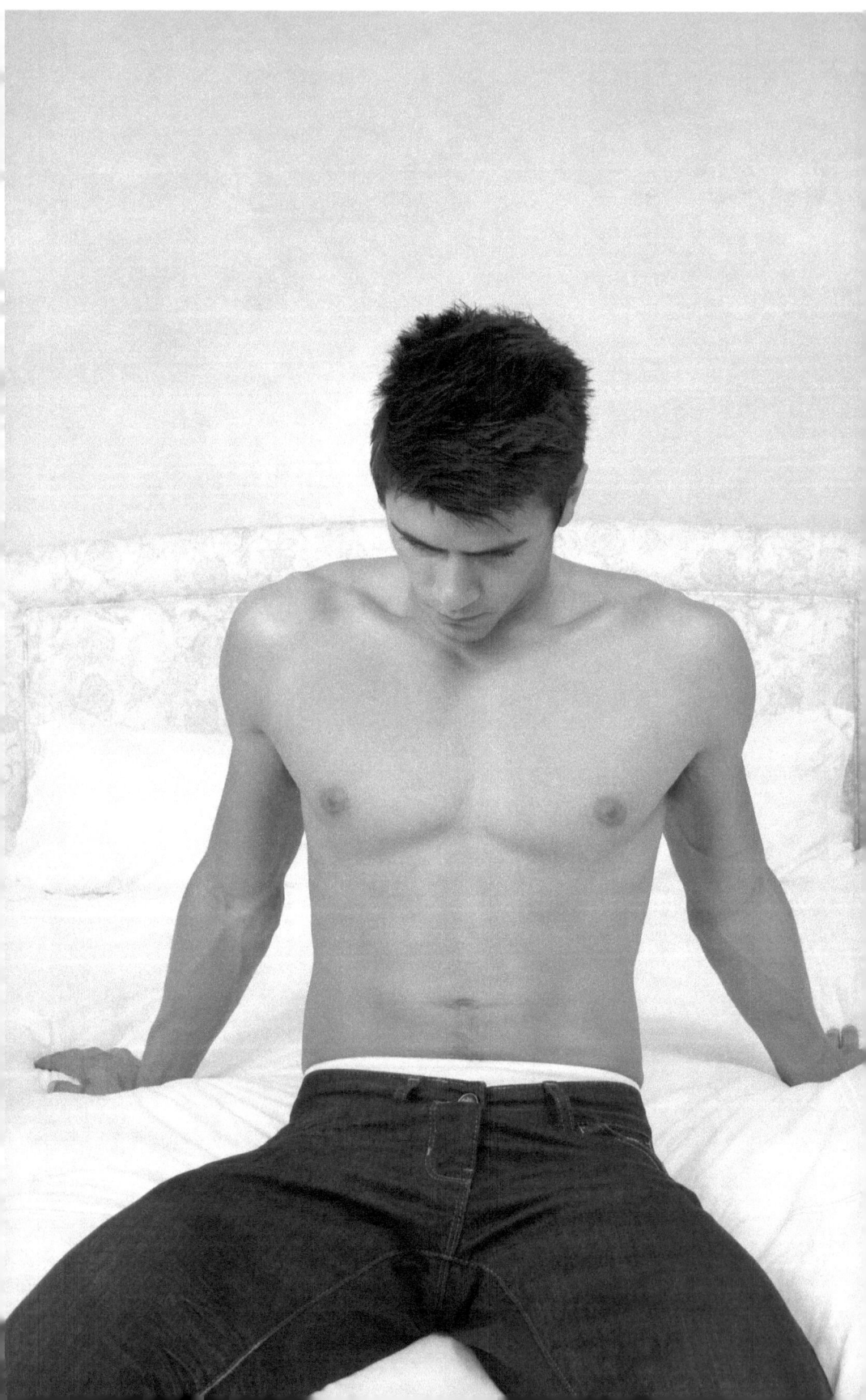

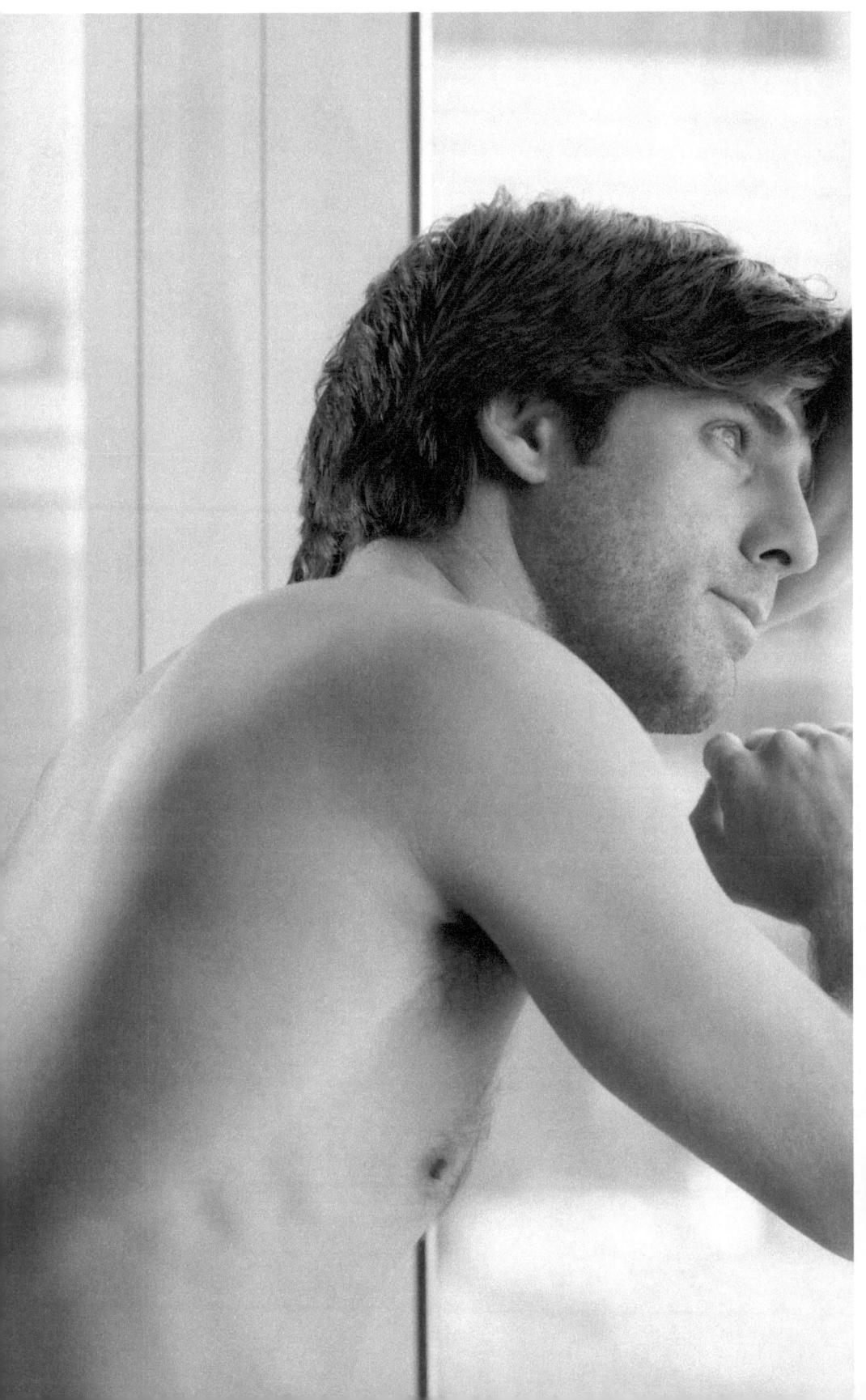

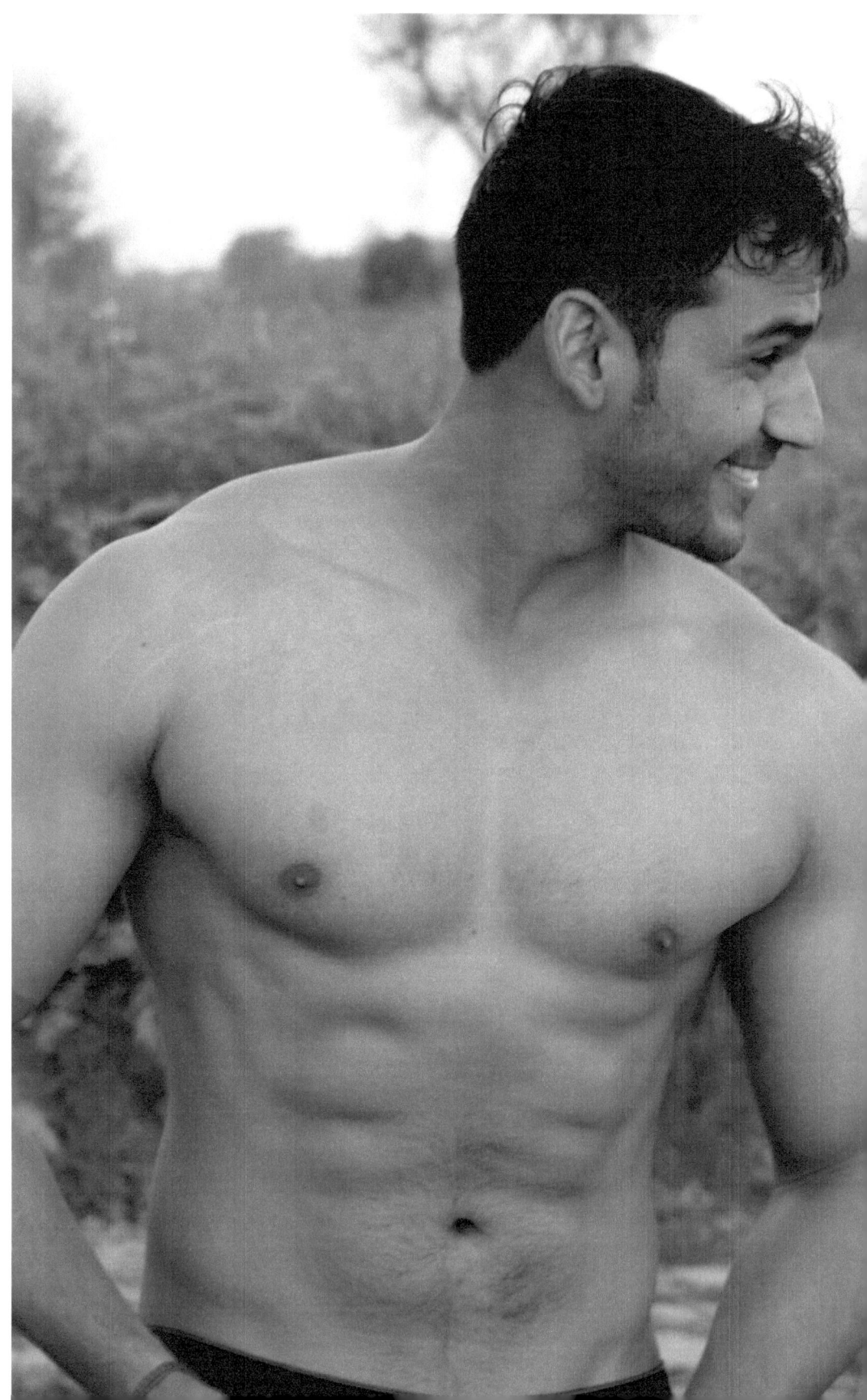

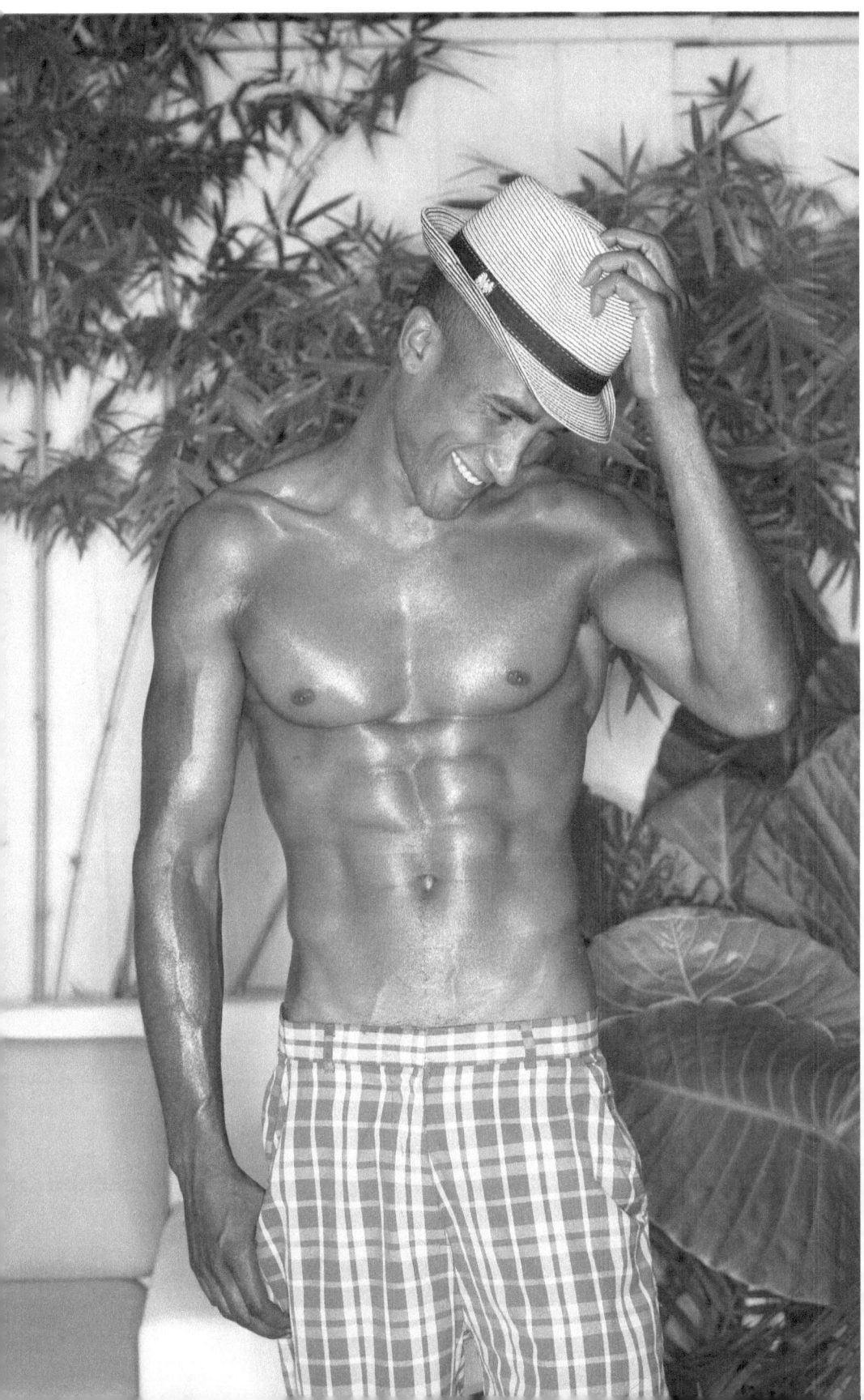

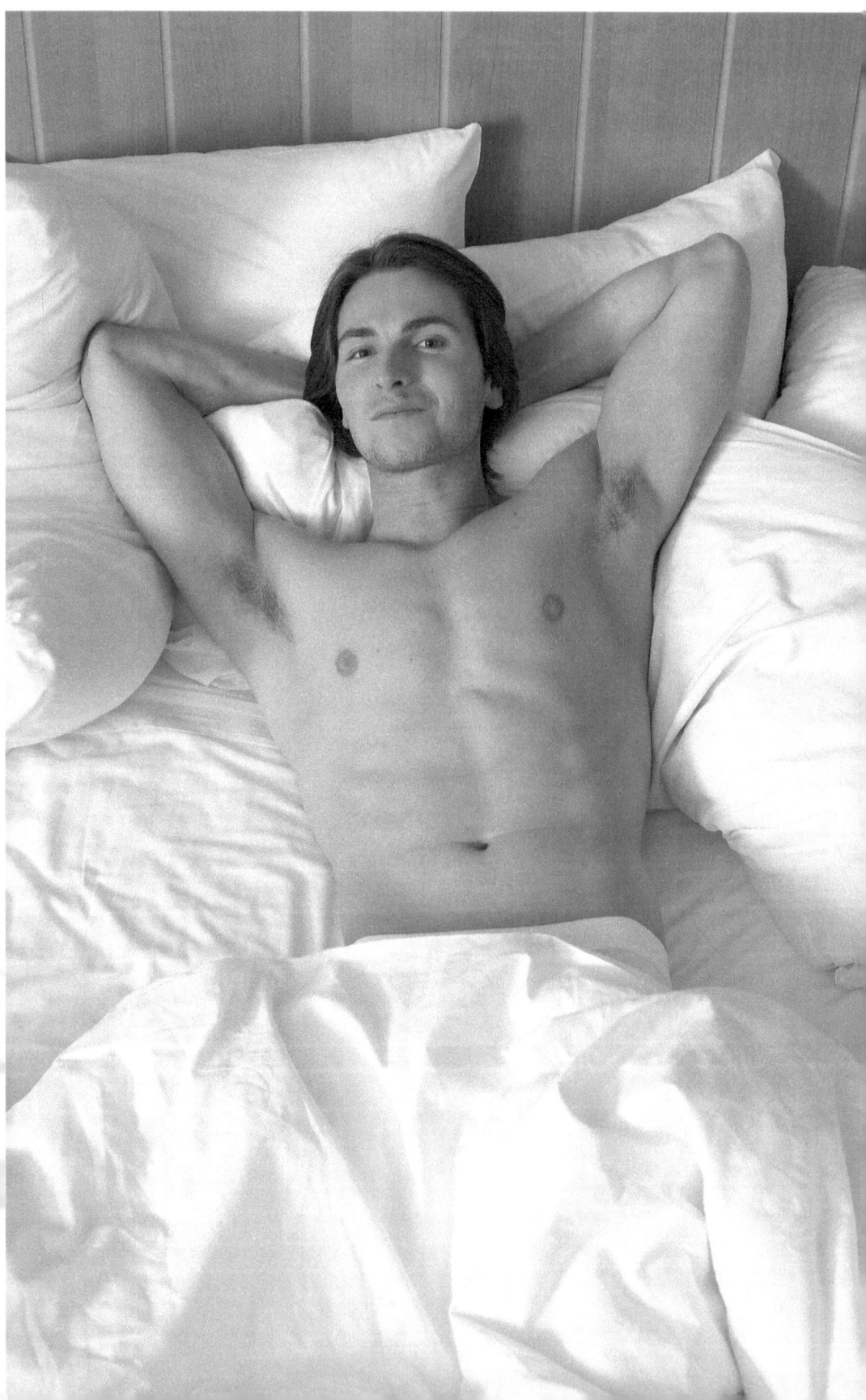

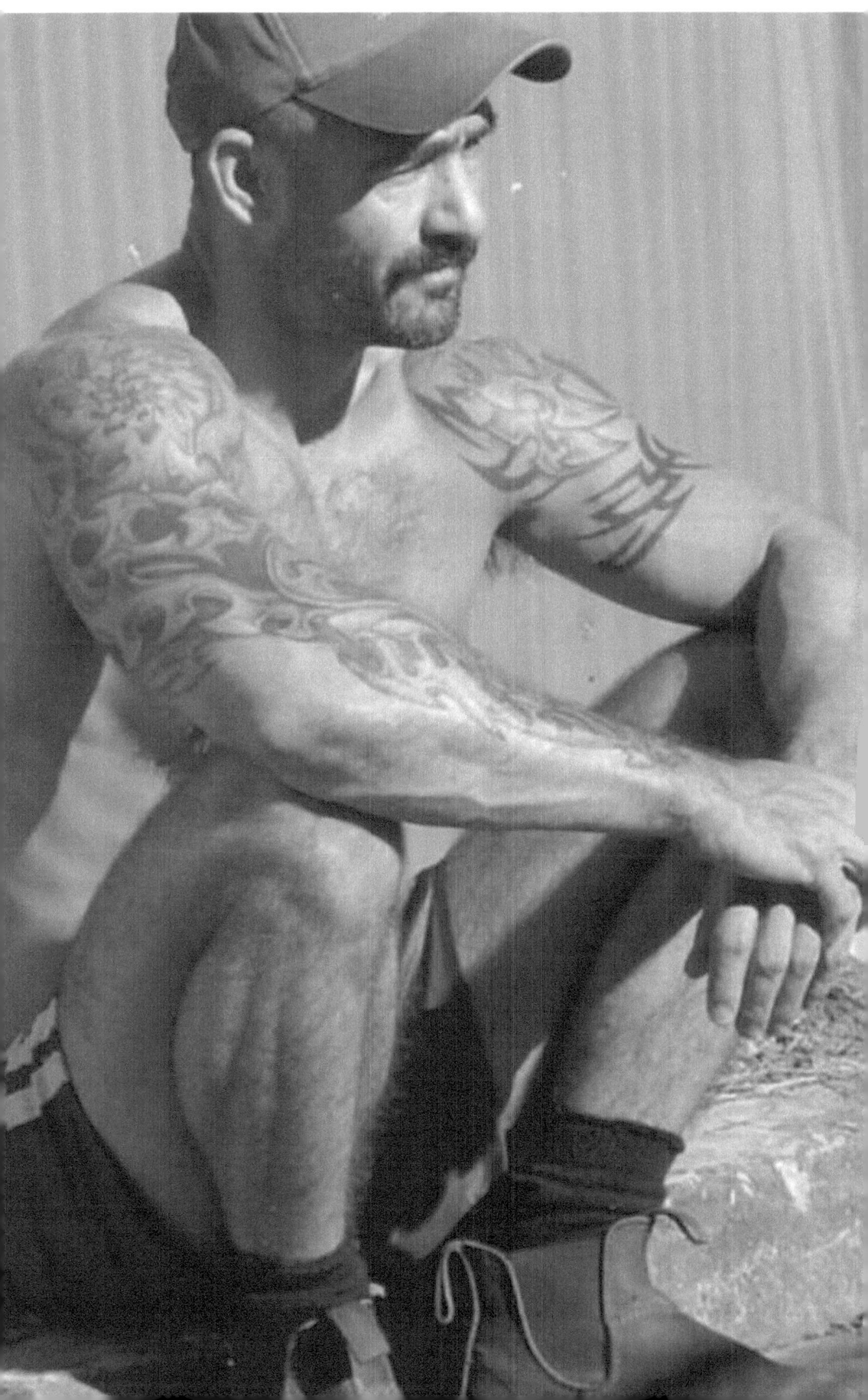

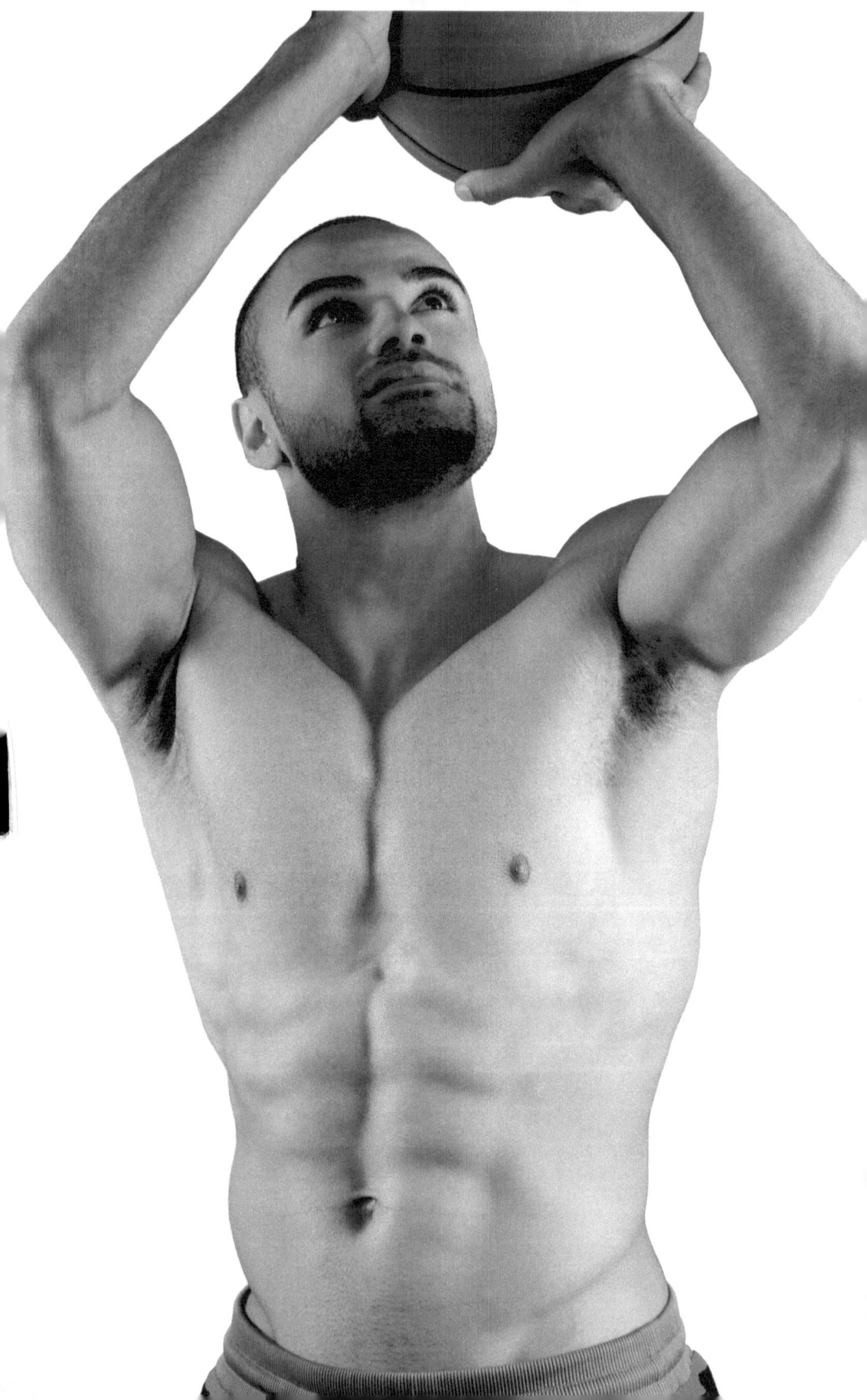

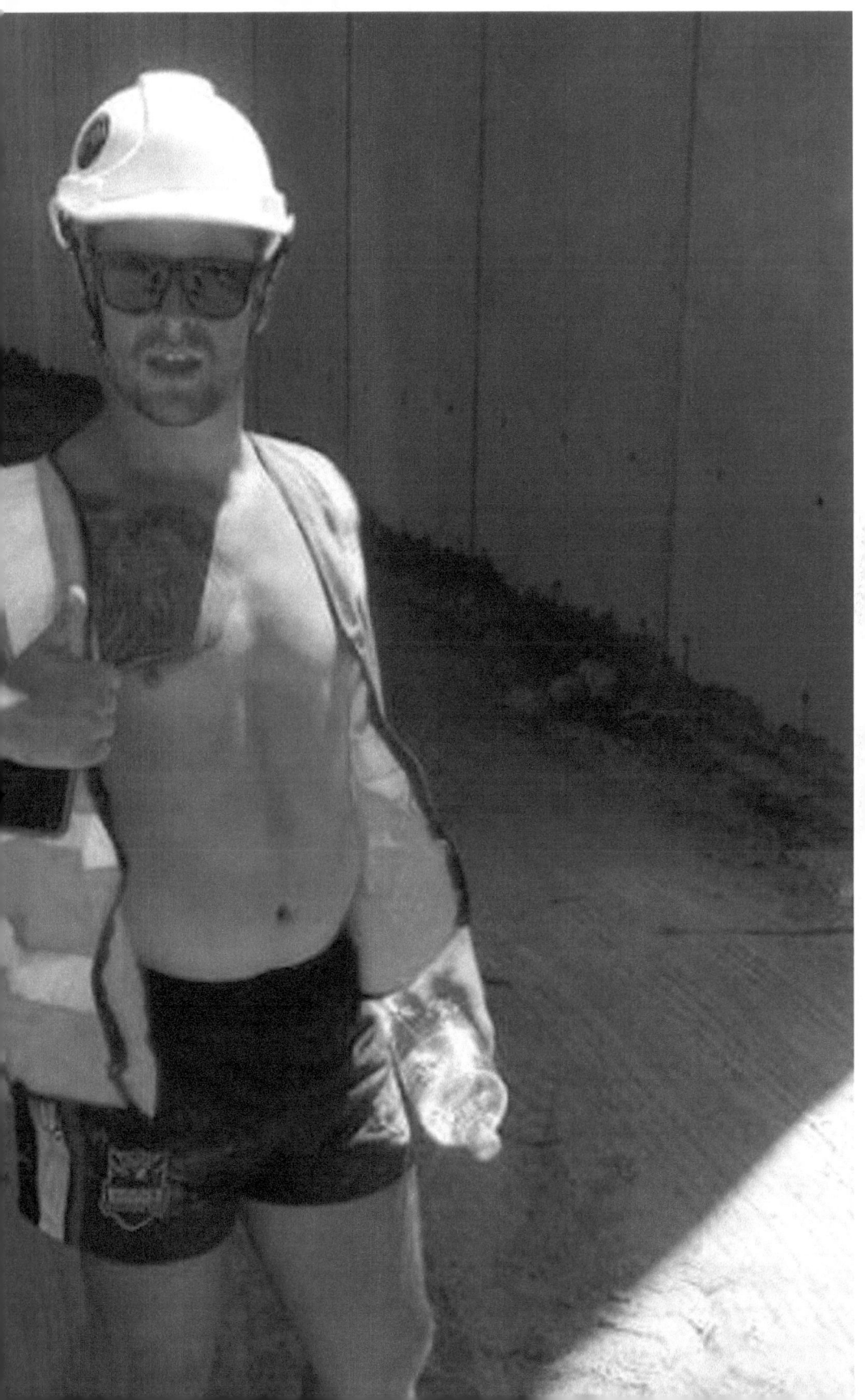

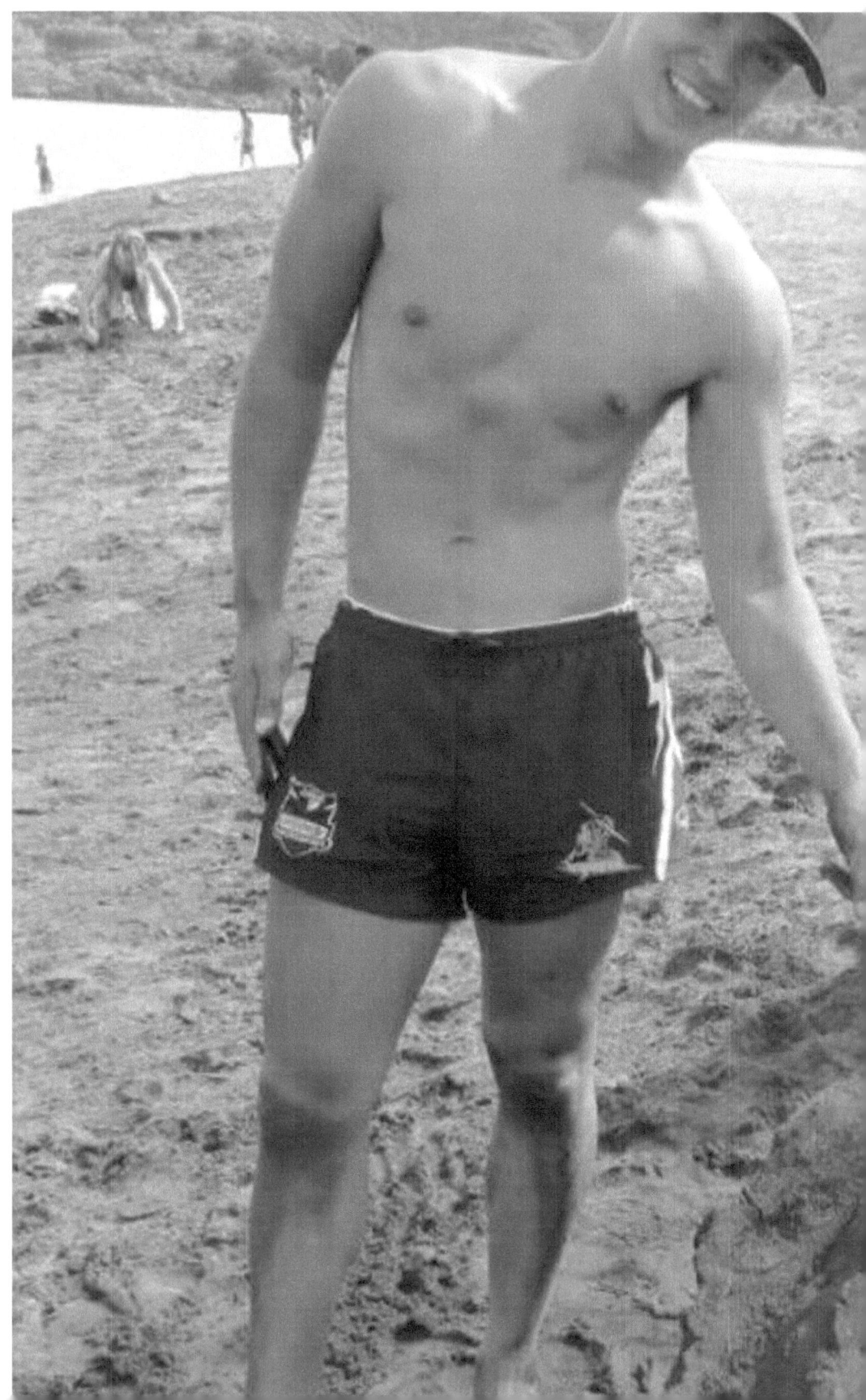

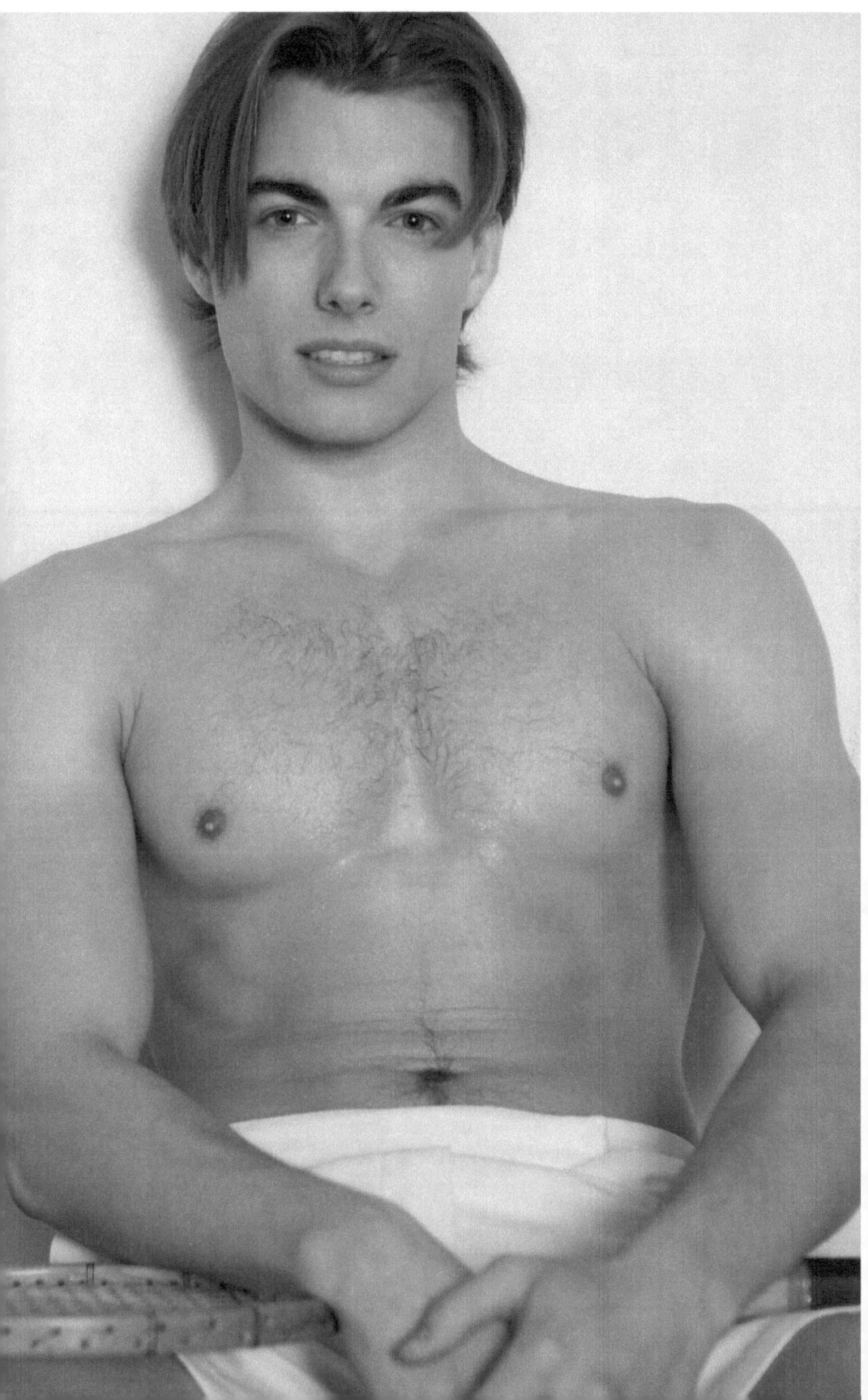

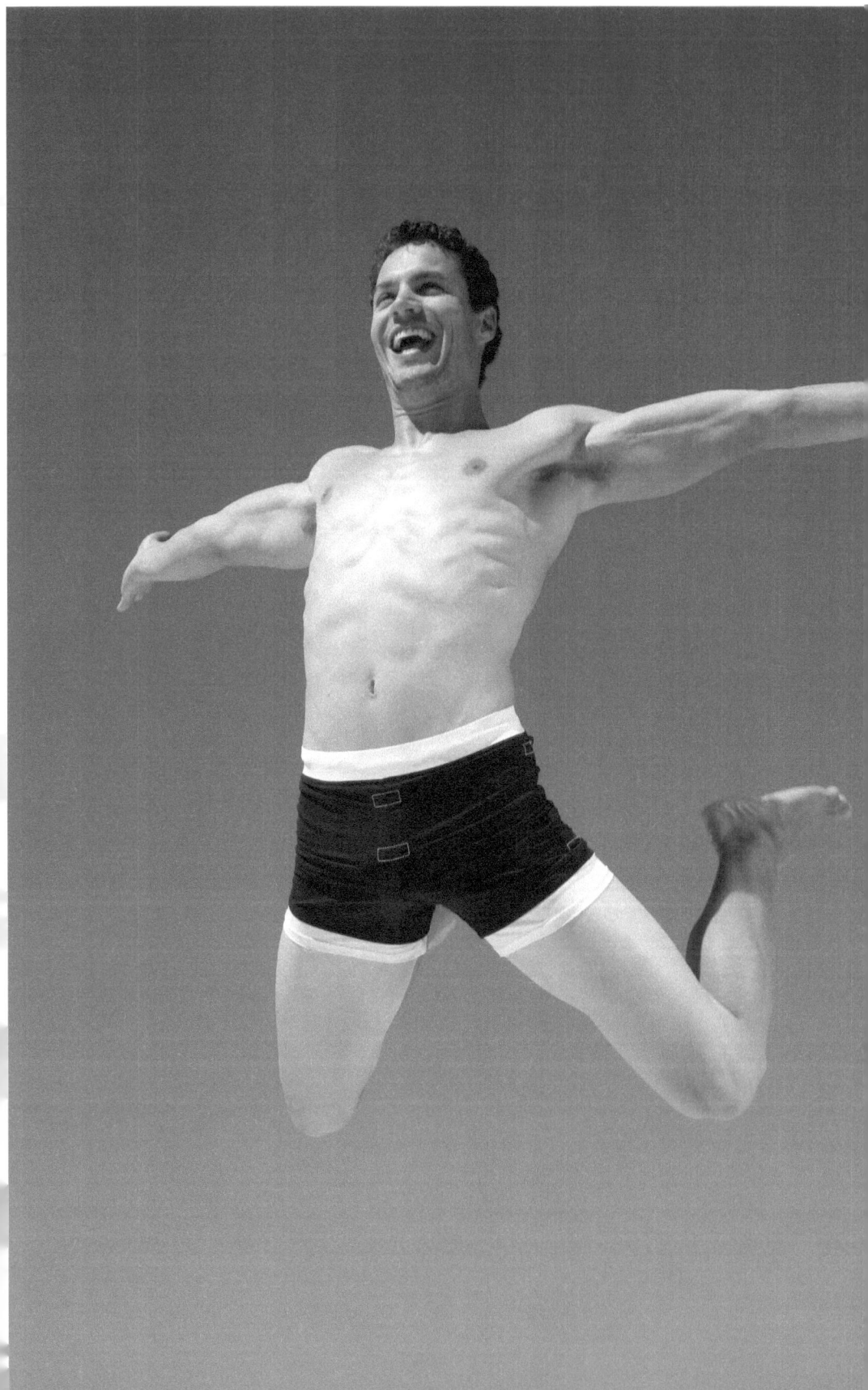

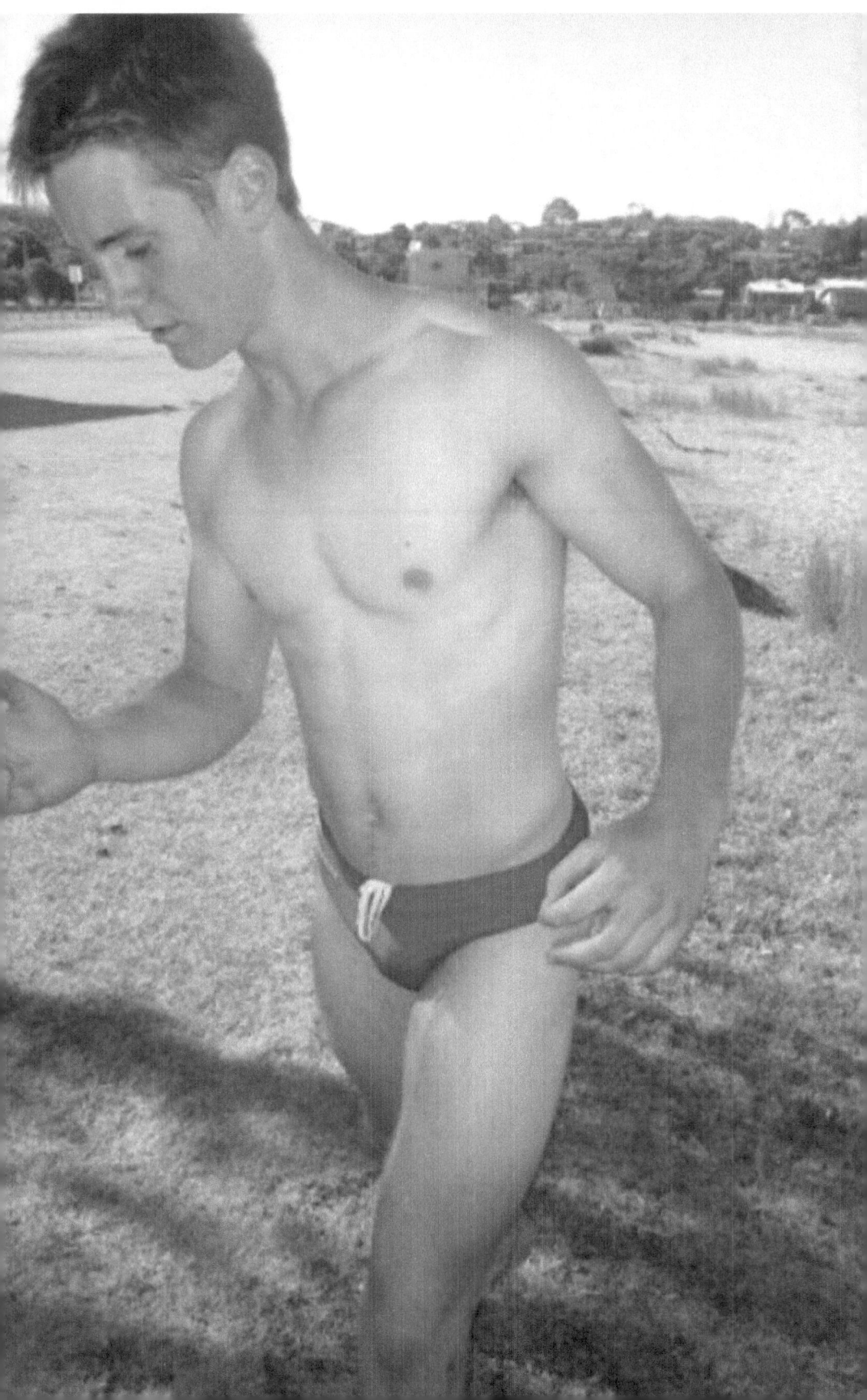

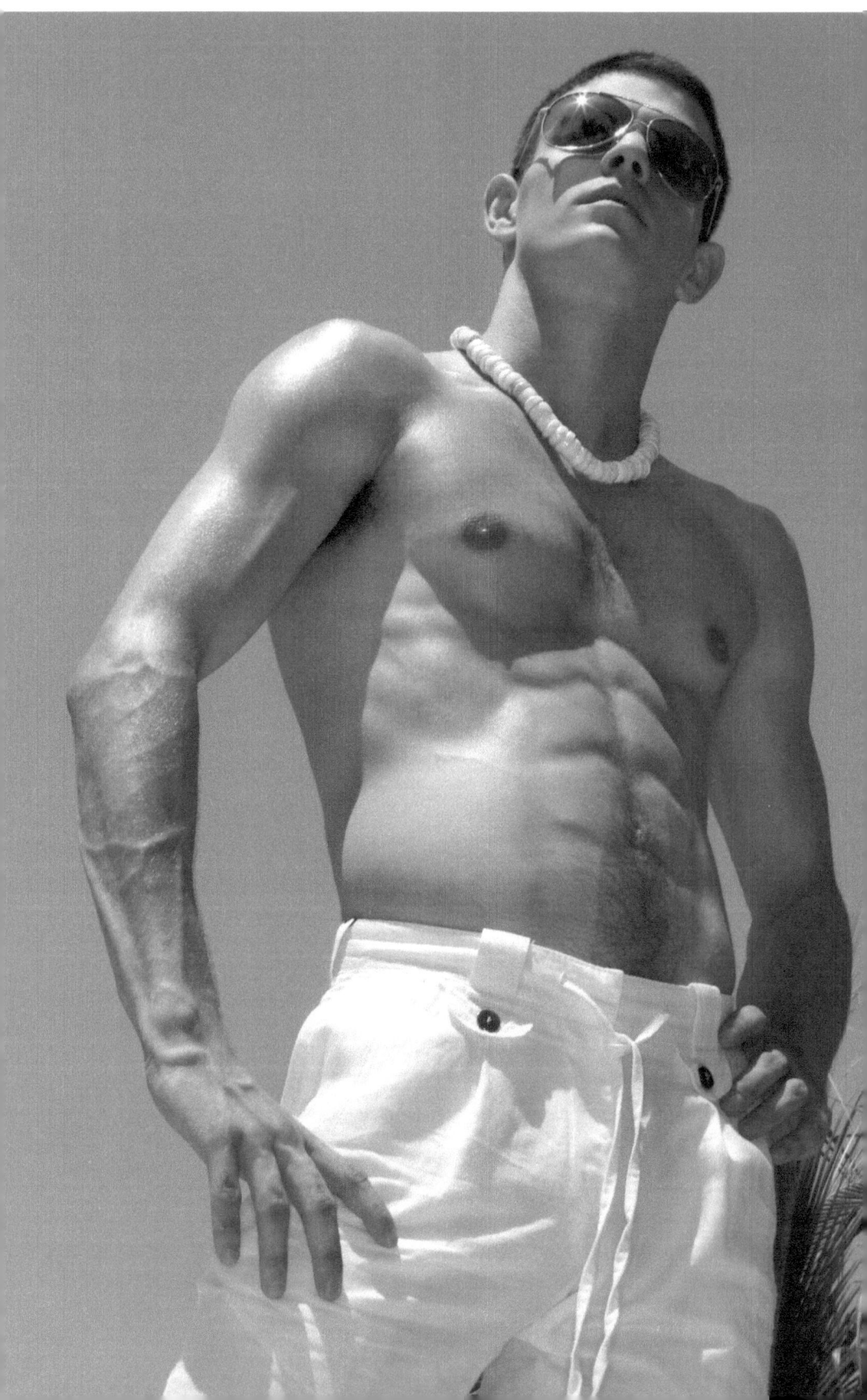

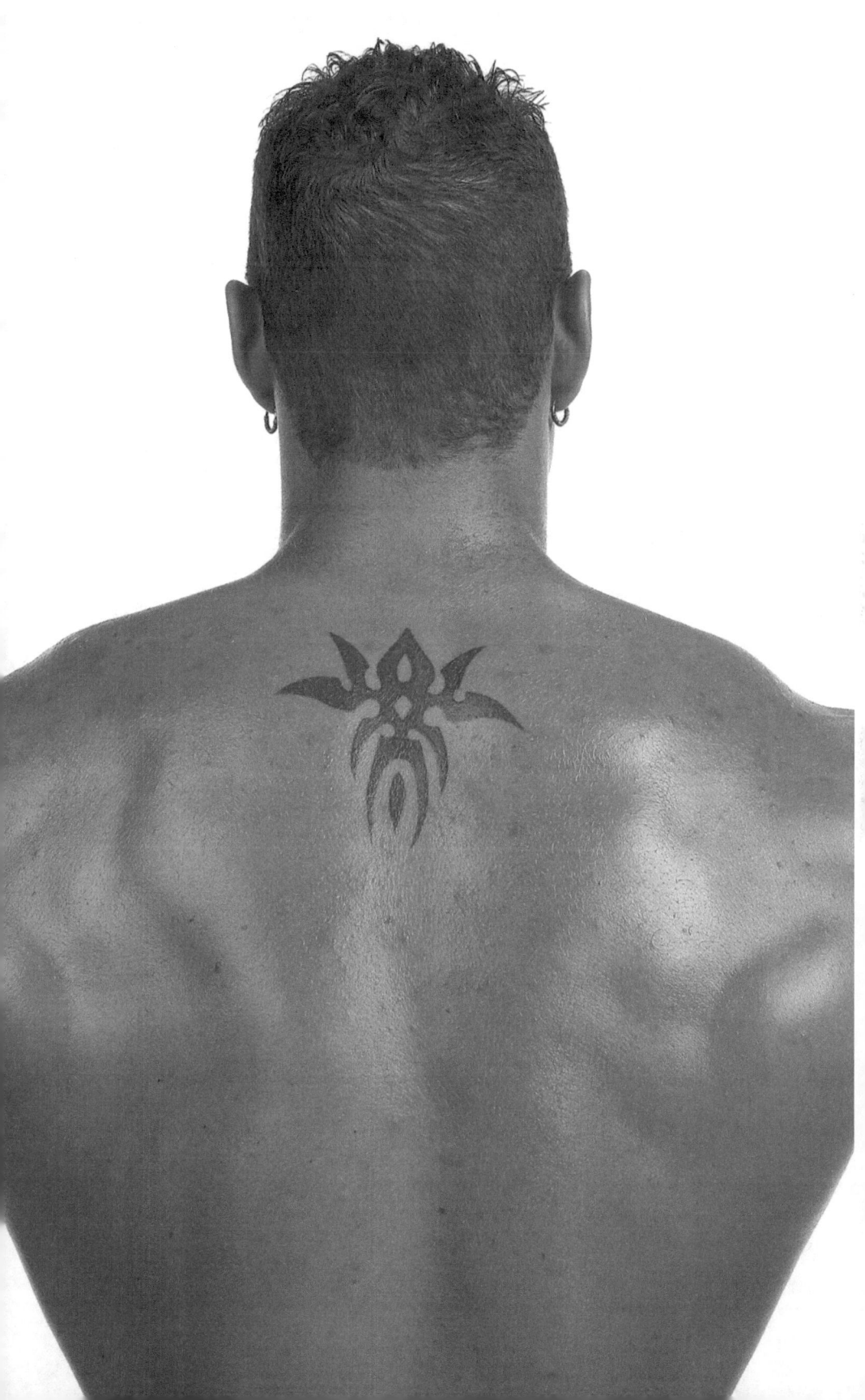

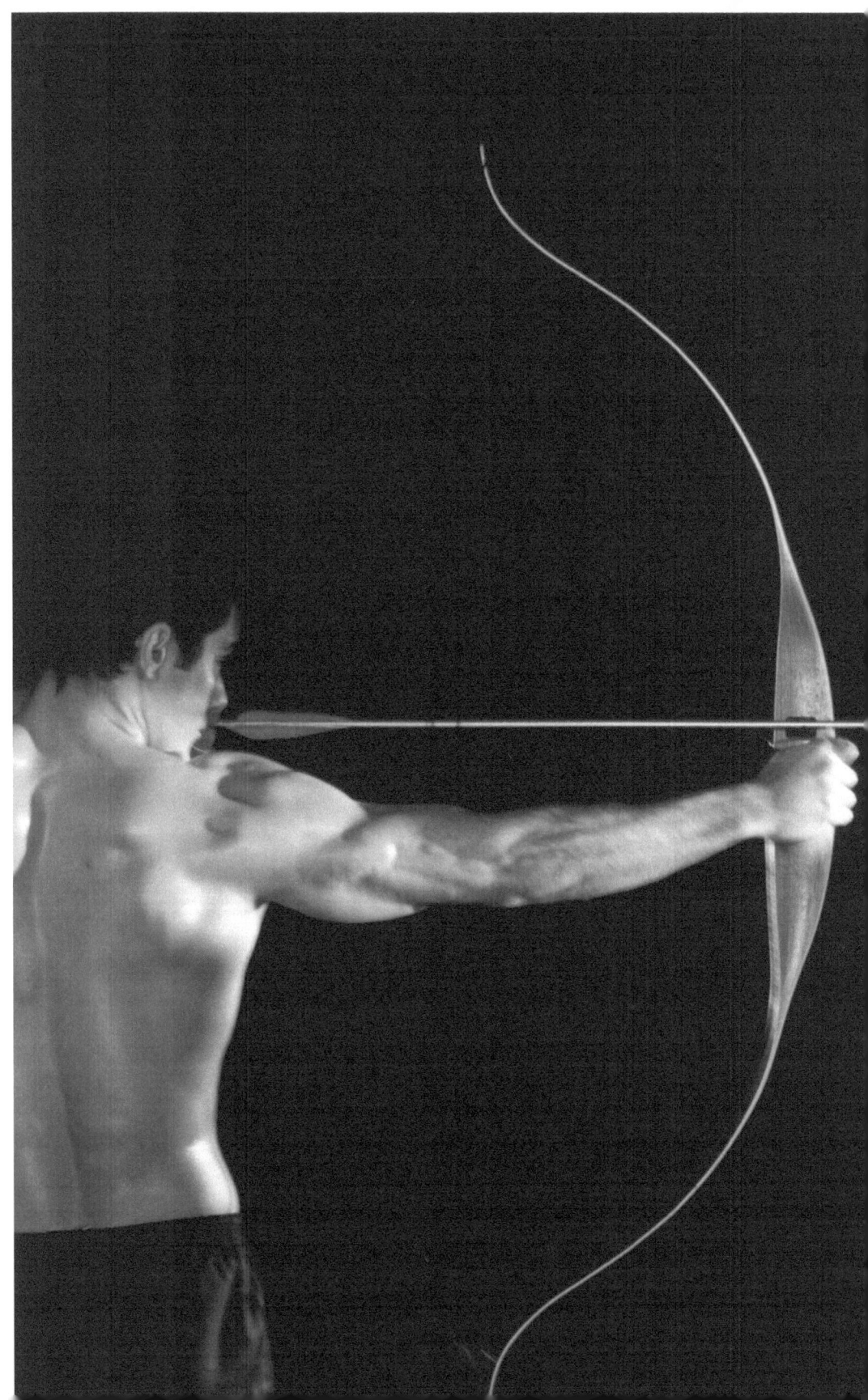

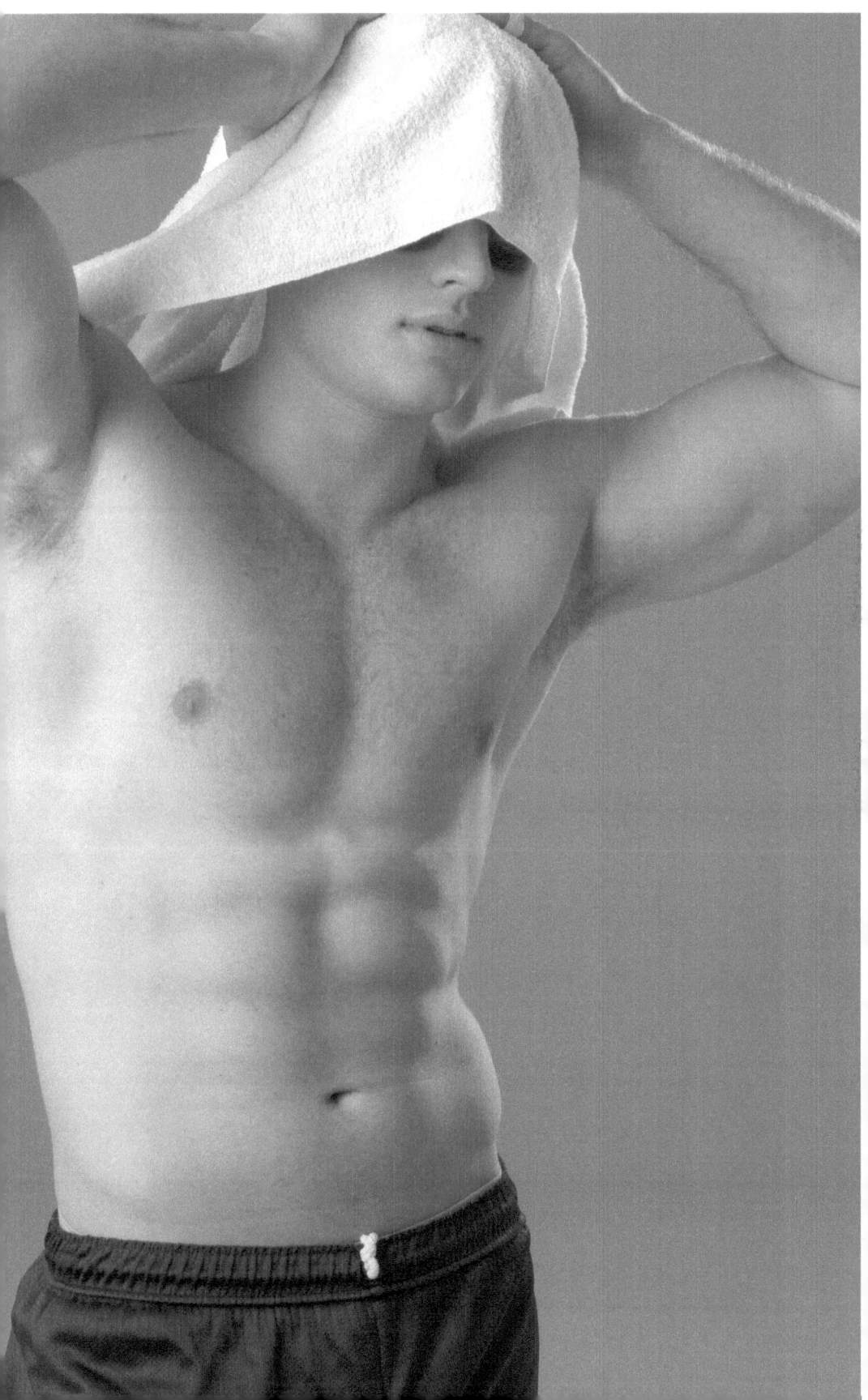

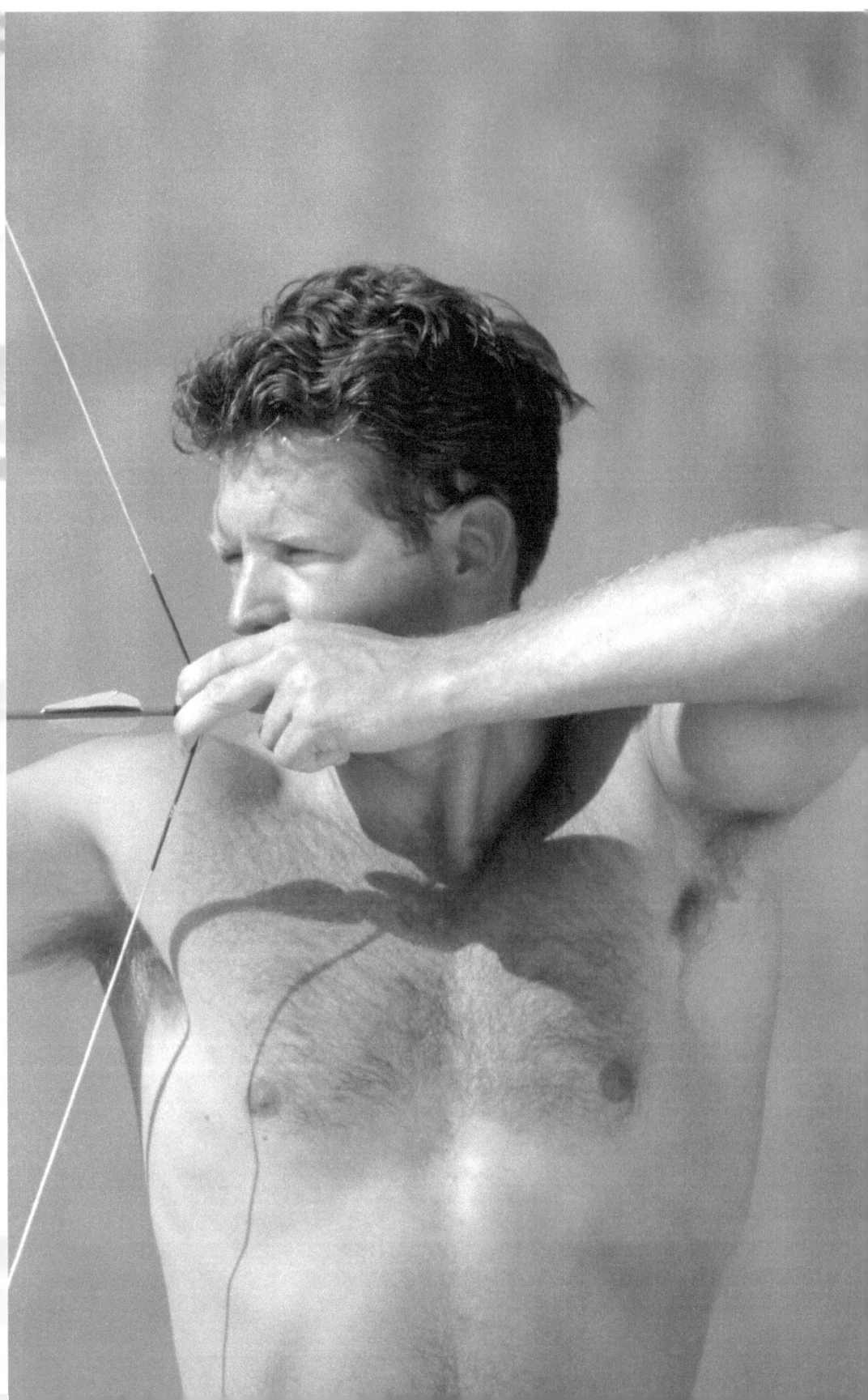

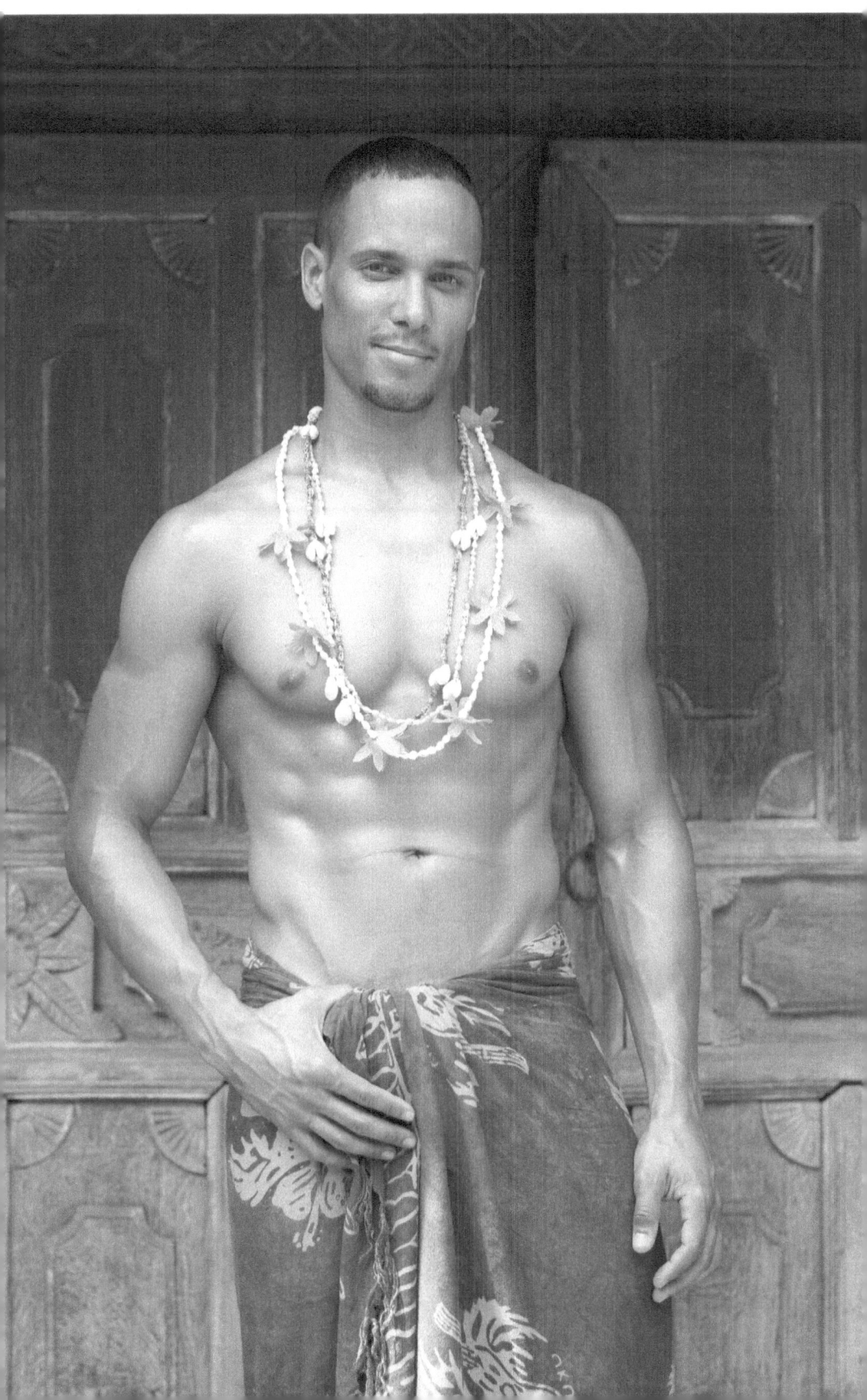

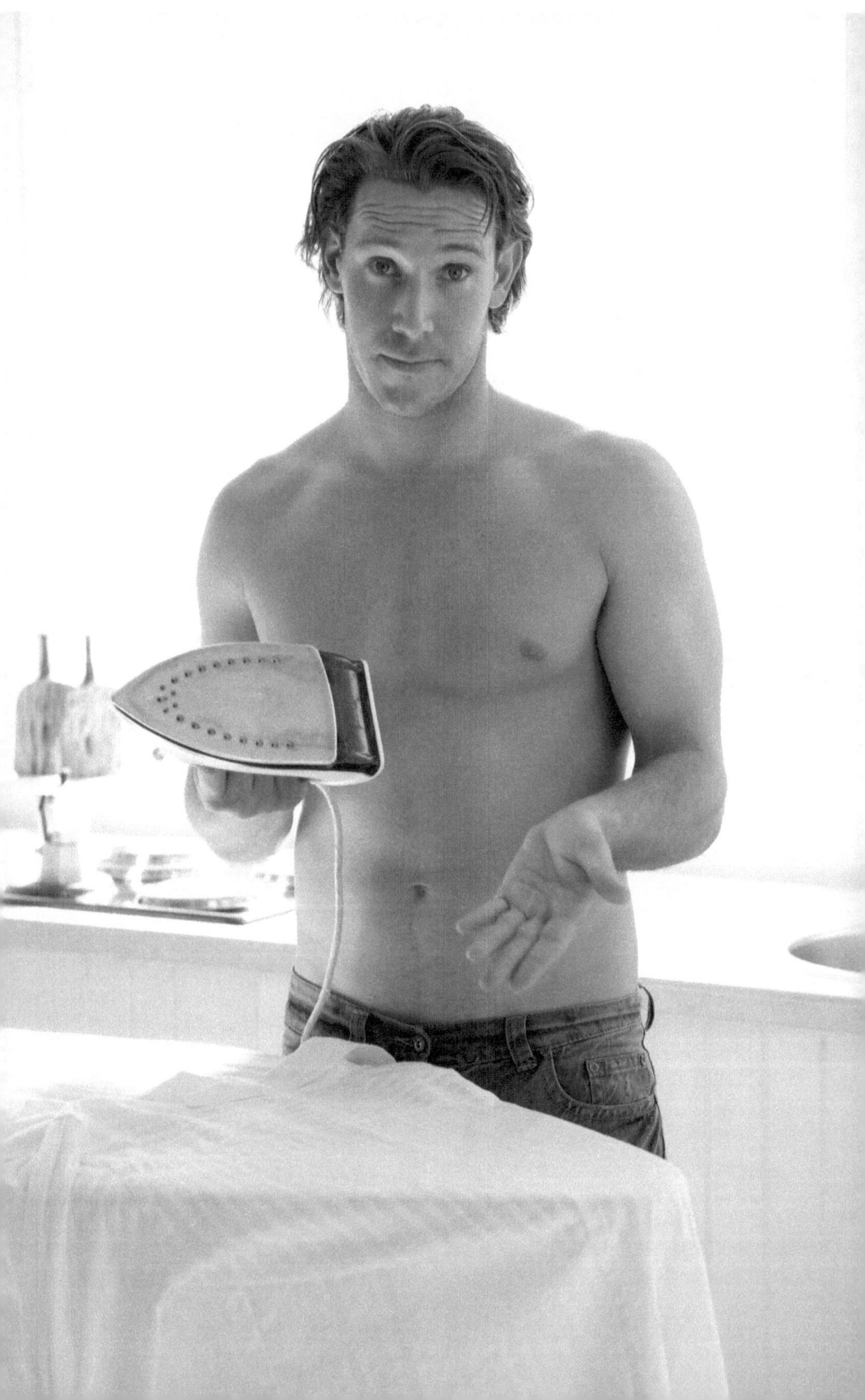

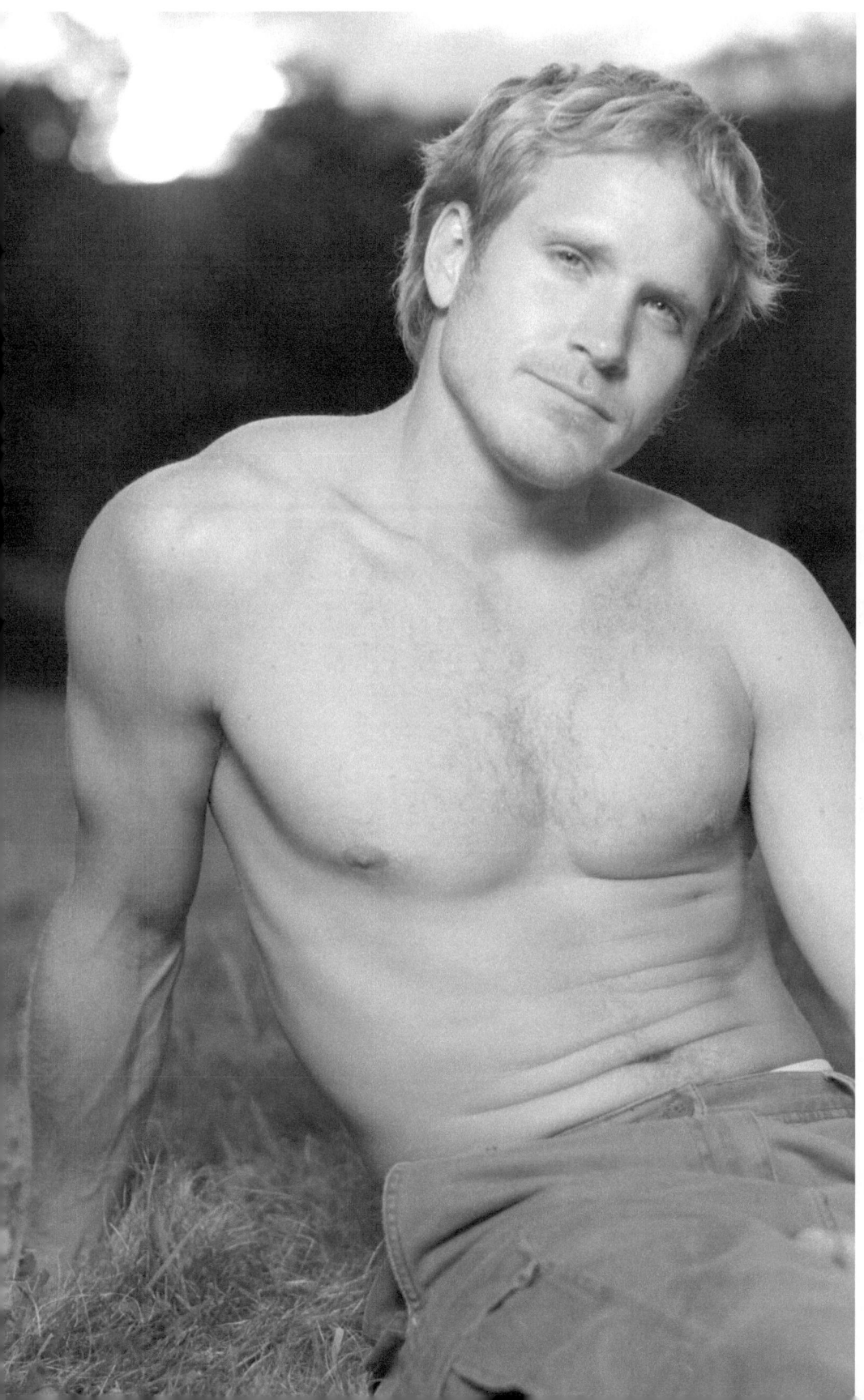

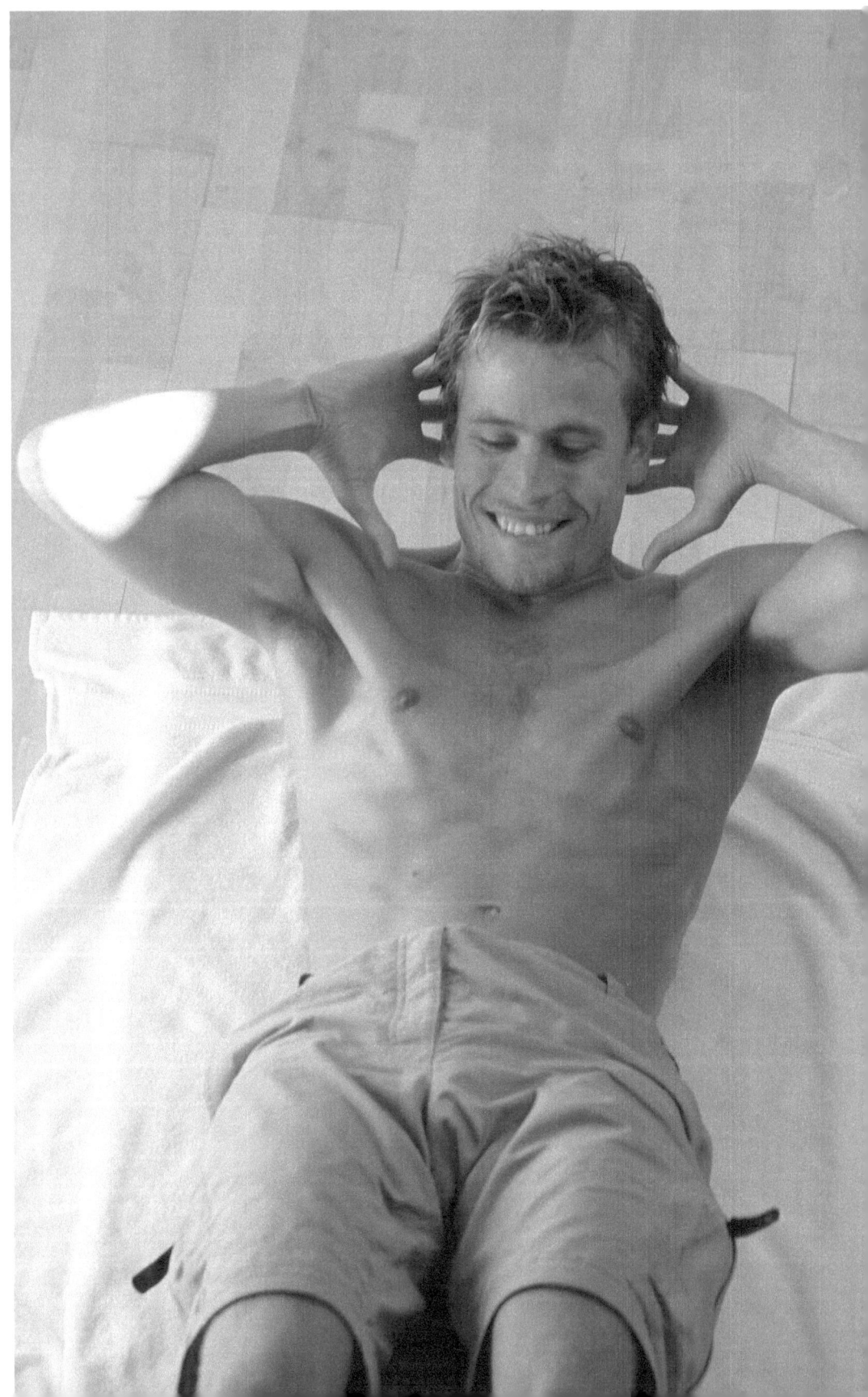

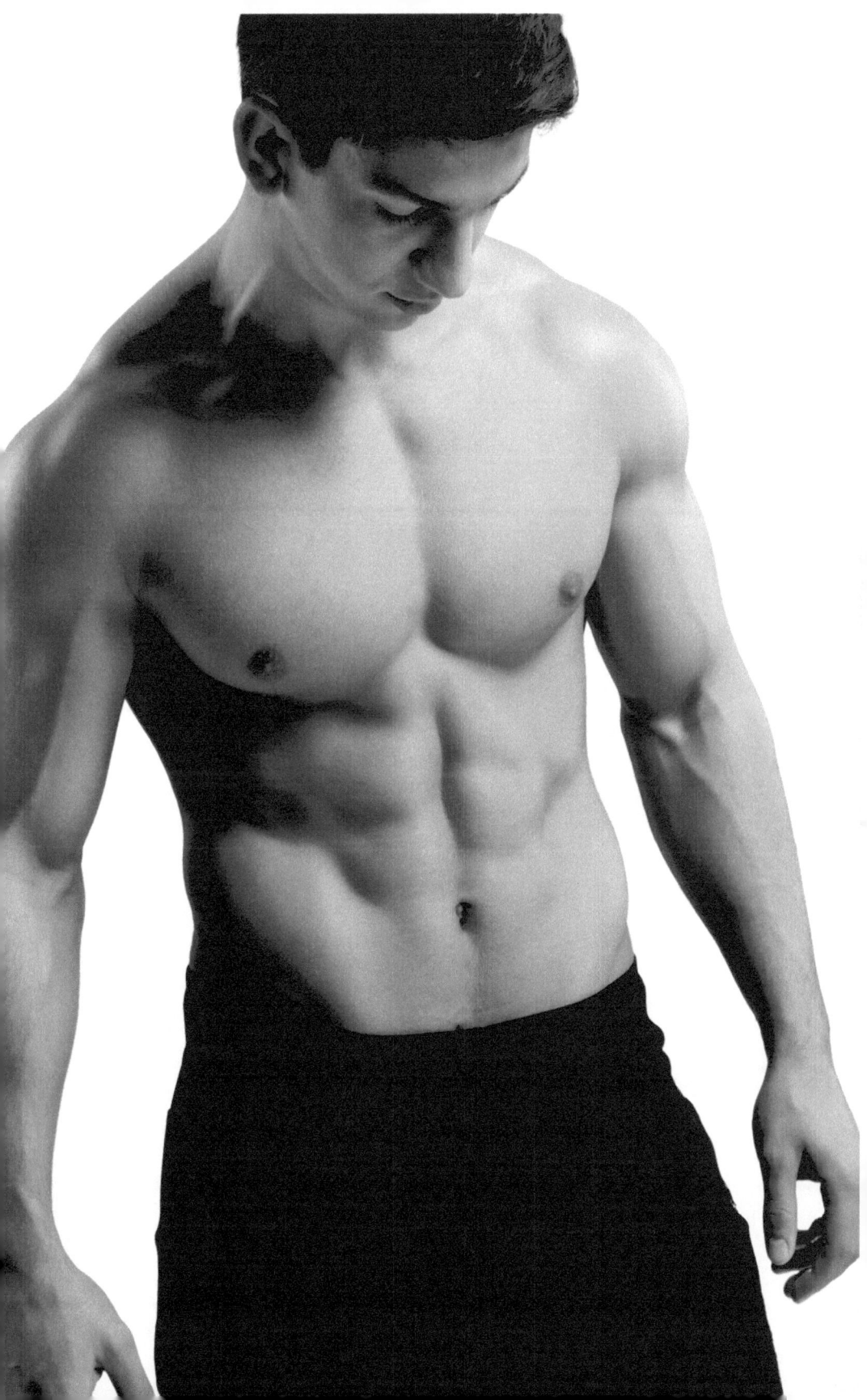

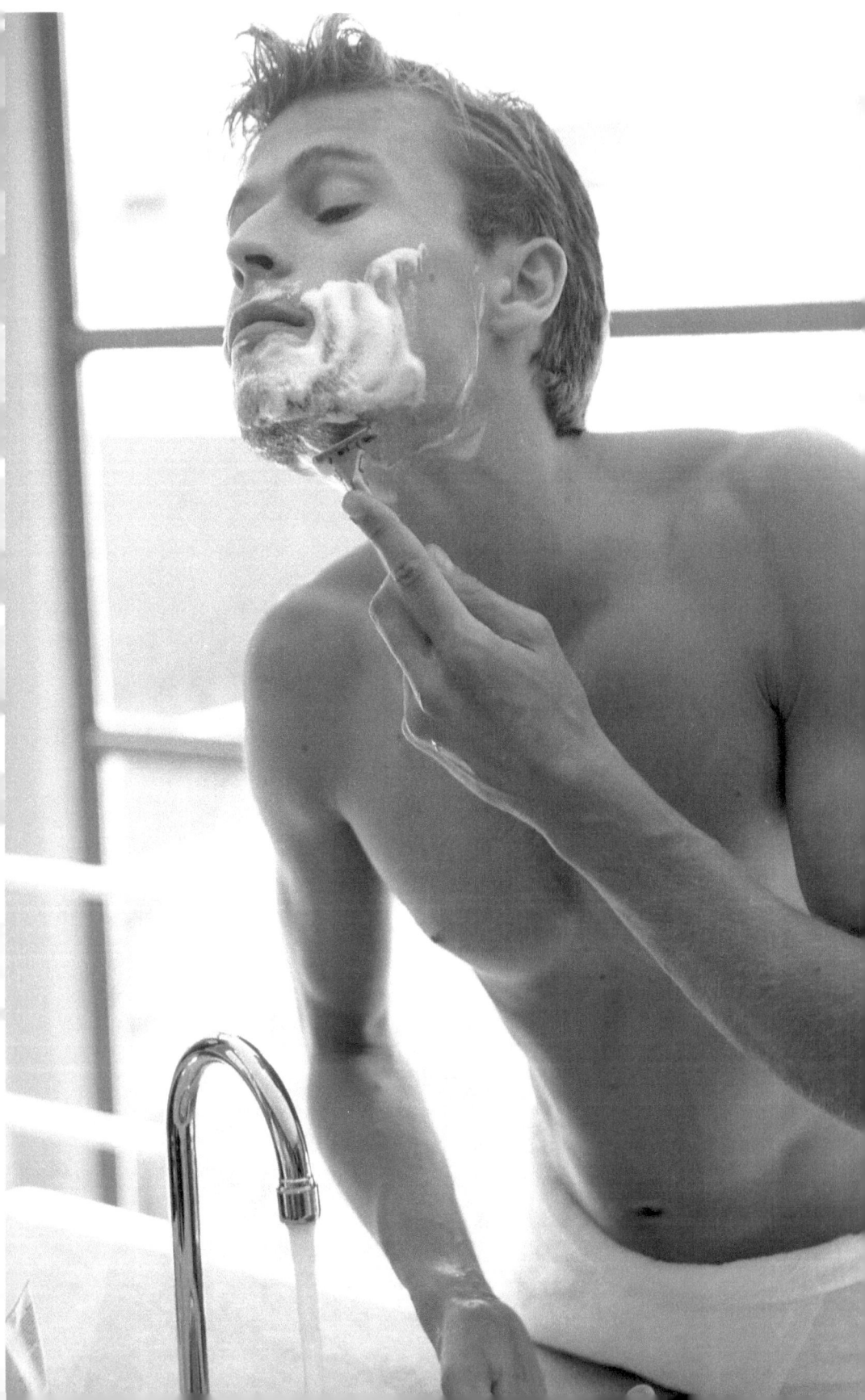

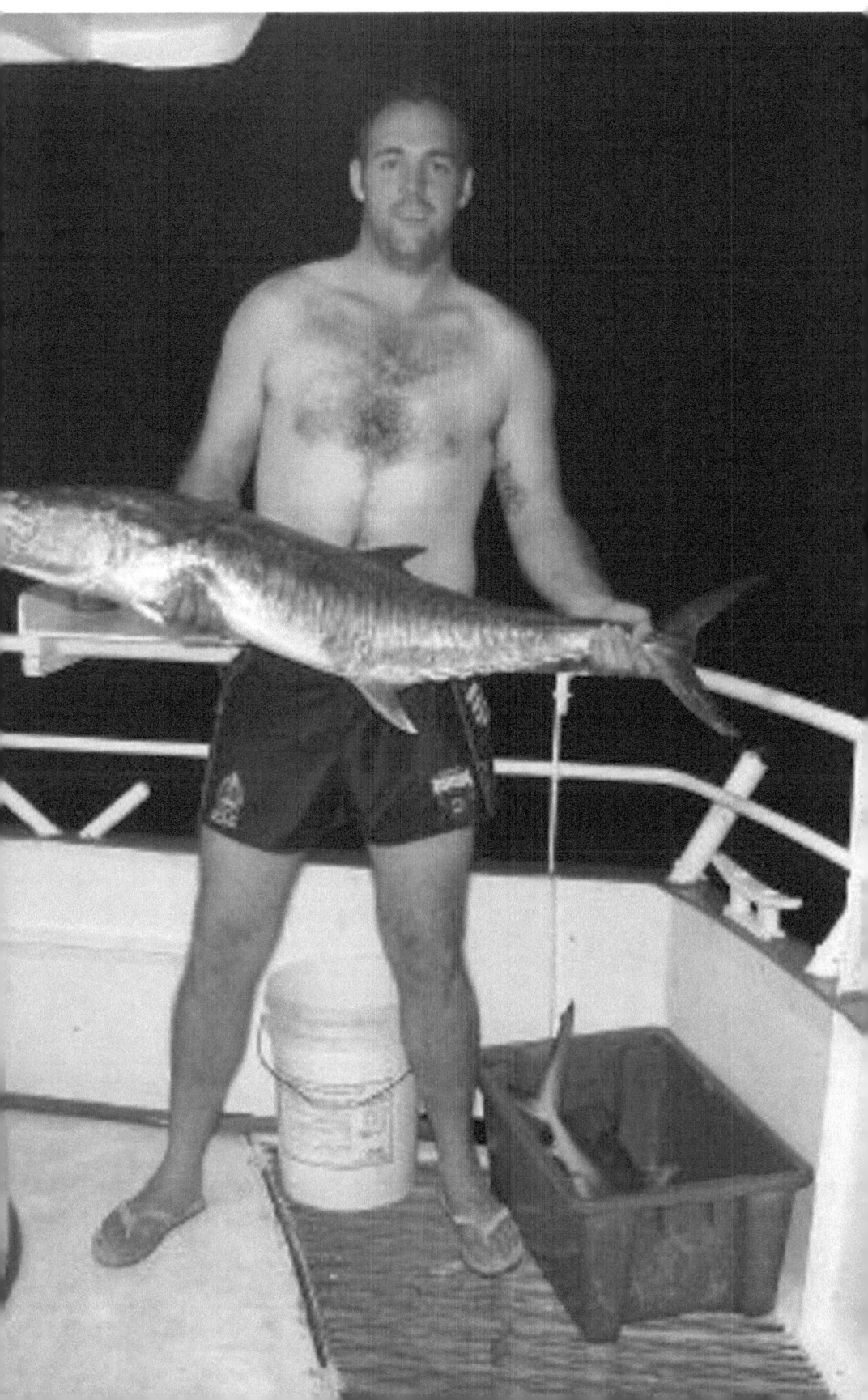

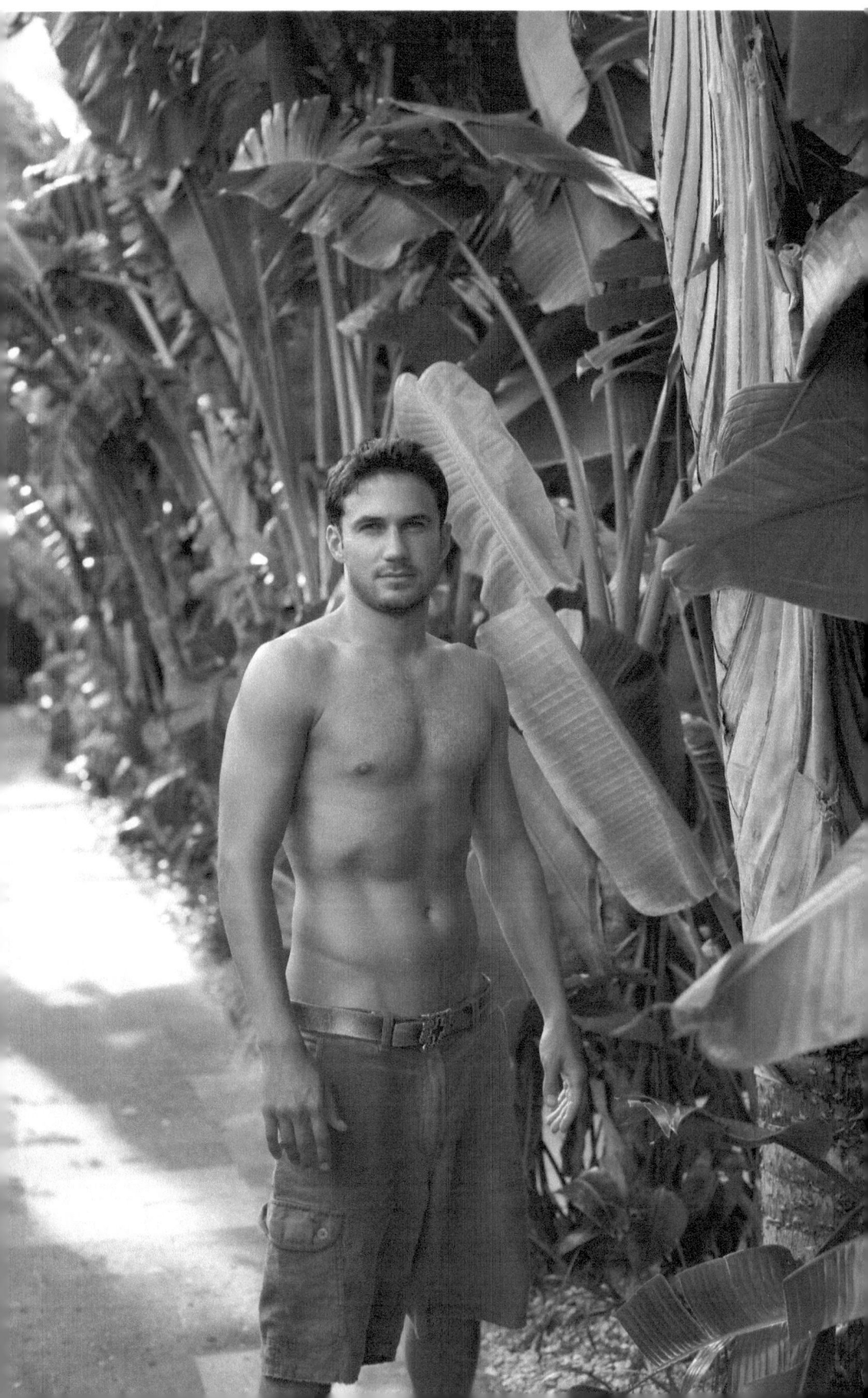

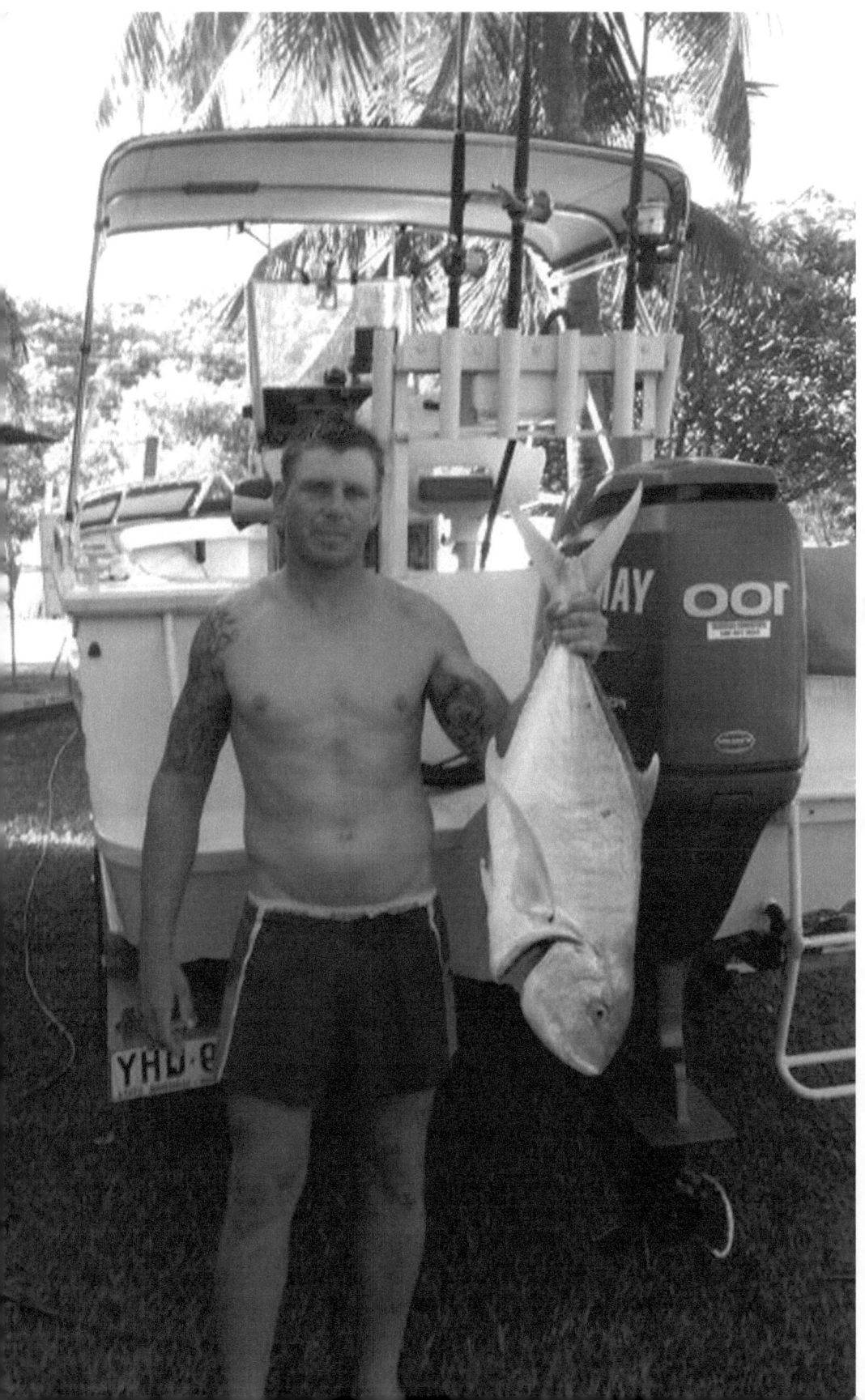

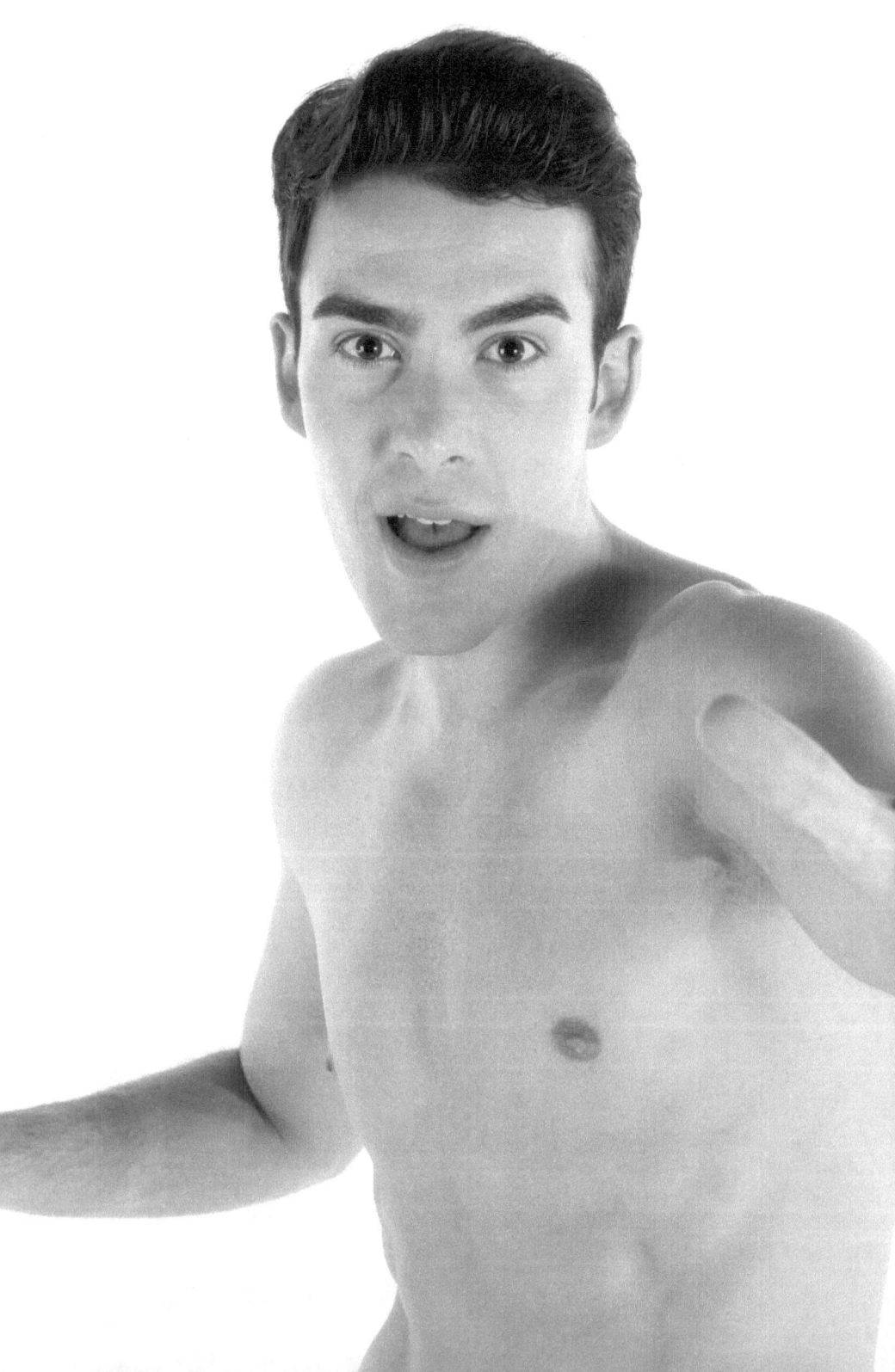

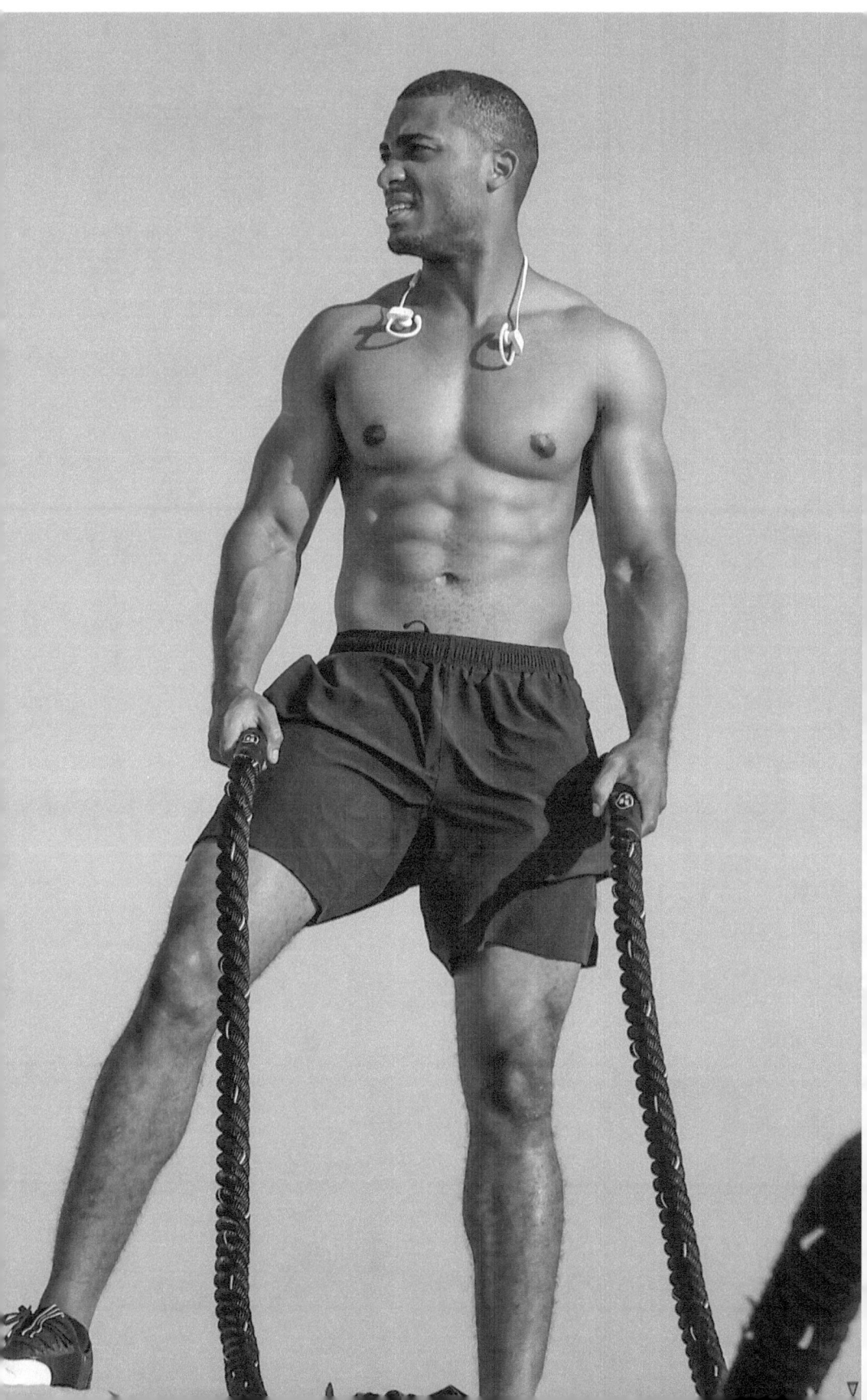

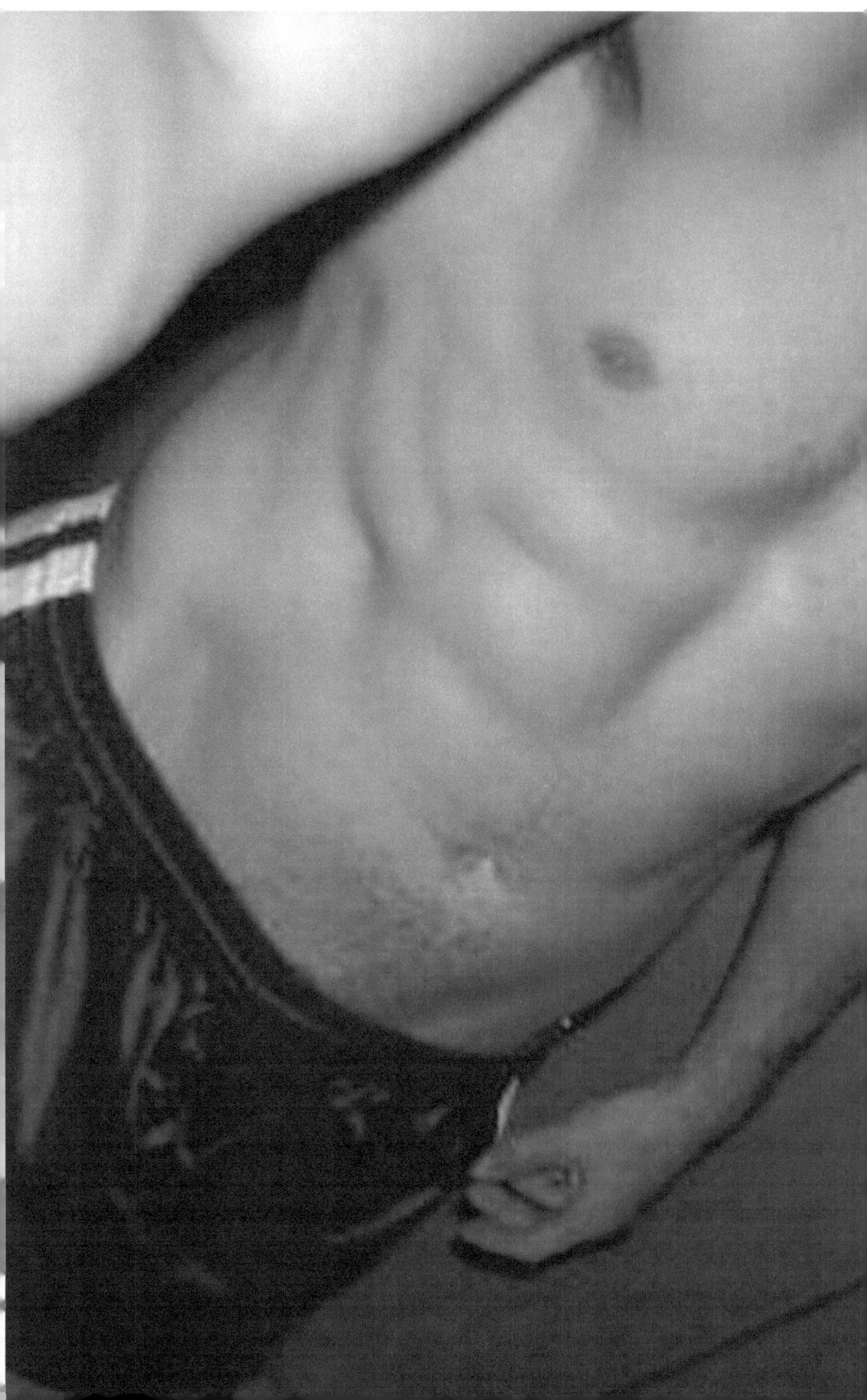

"If I had a great body, I'd be naked all the time."

Claire Forlani

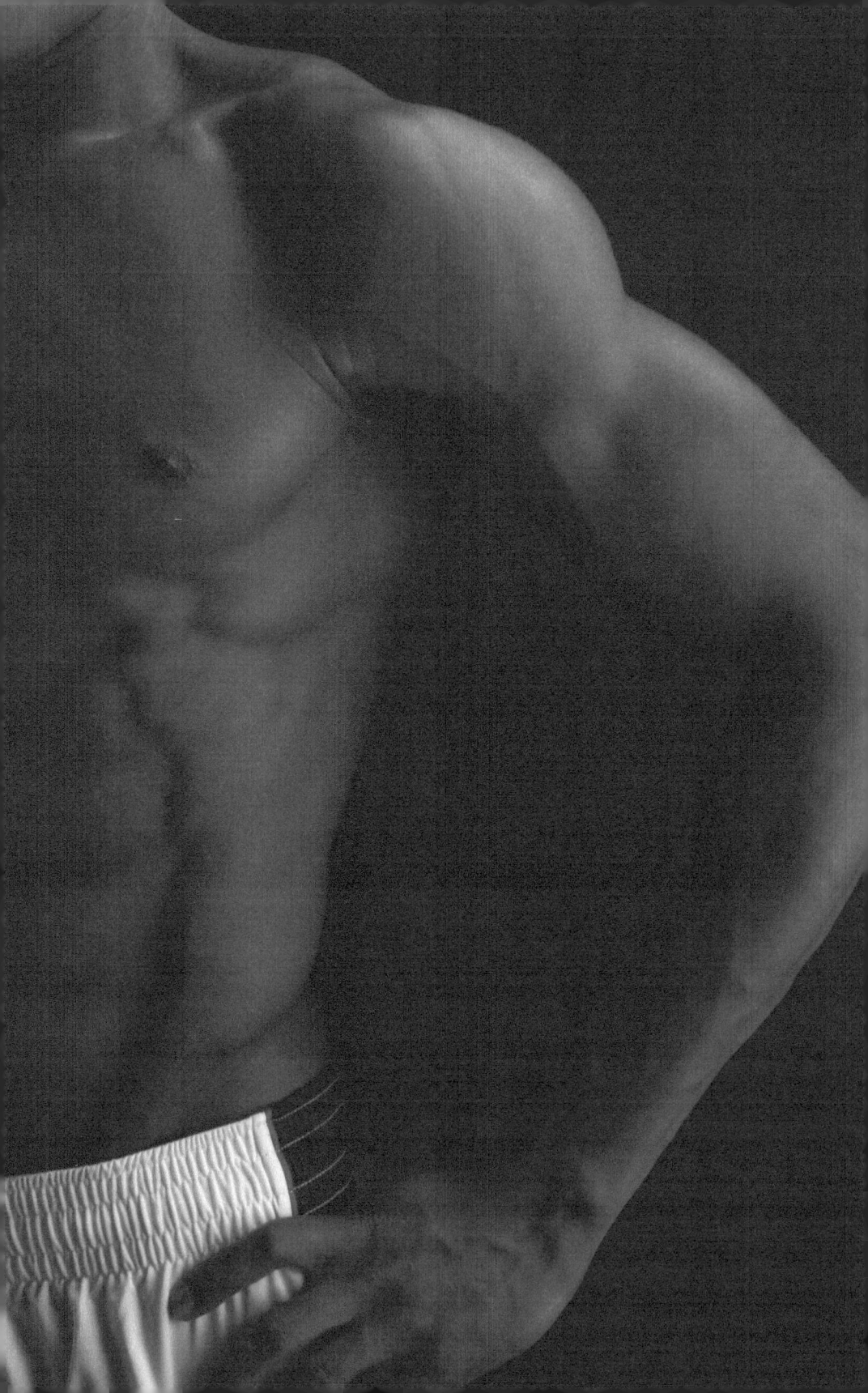

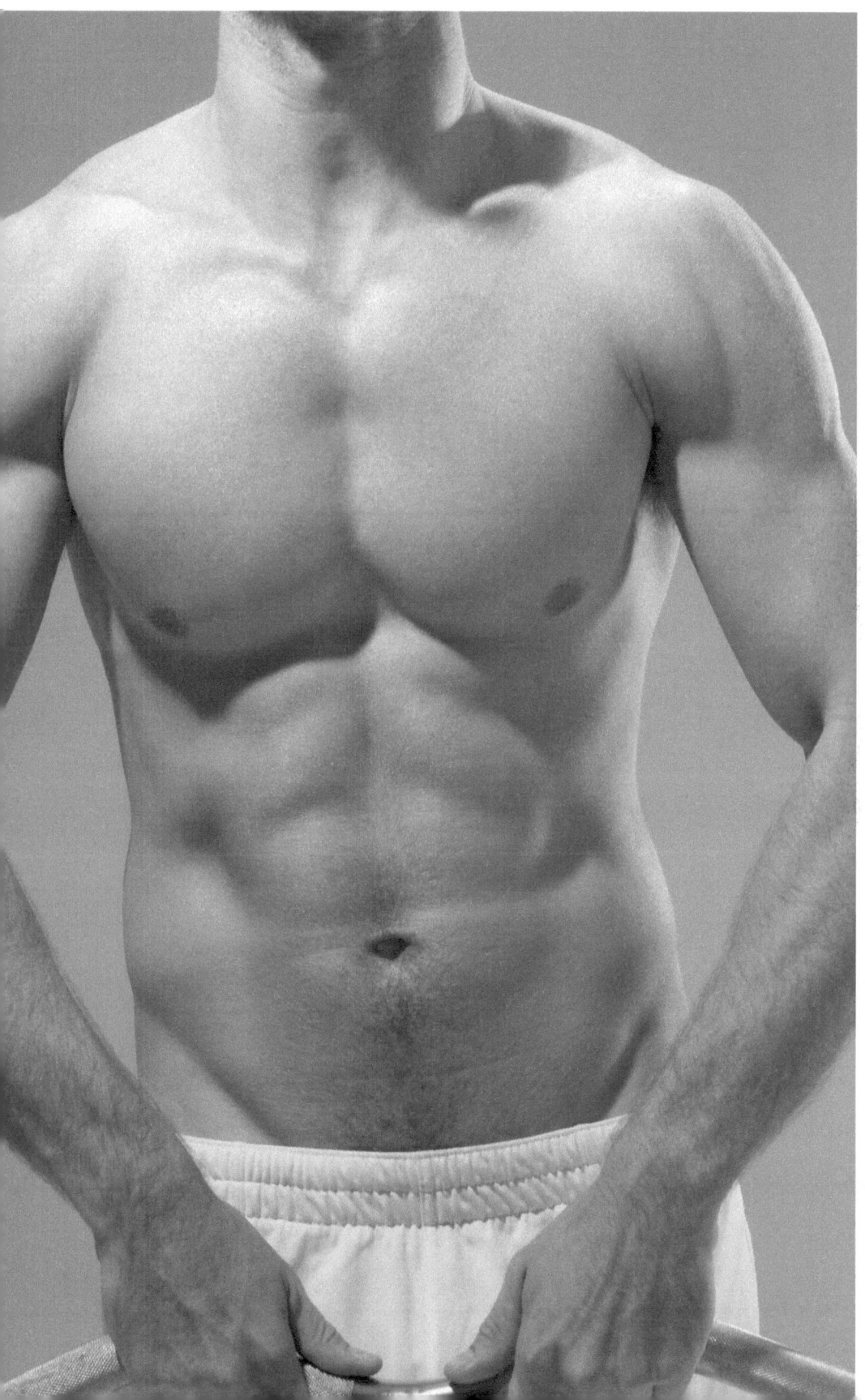

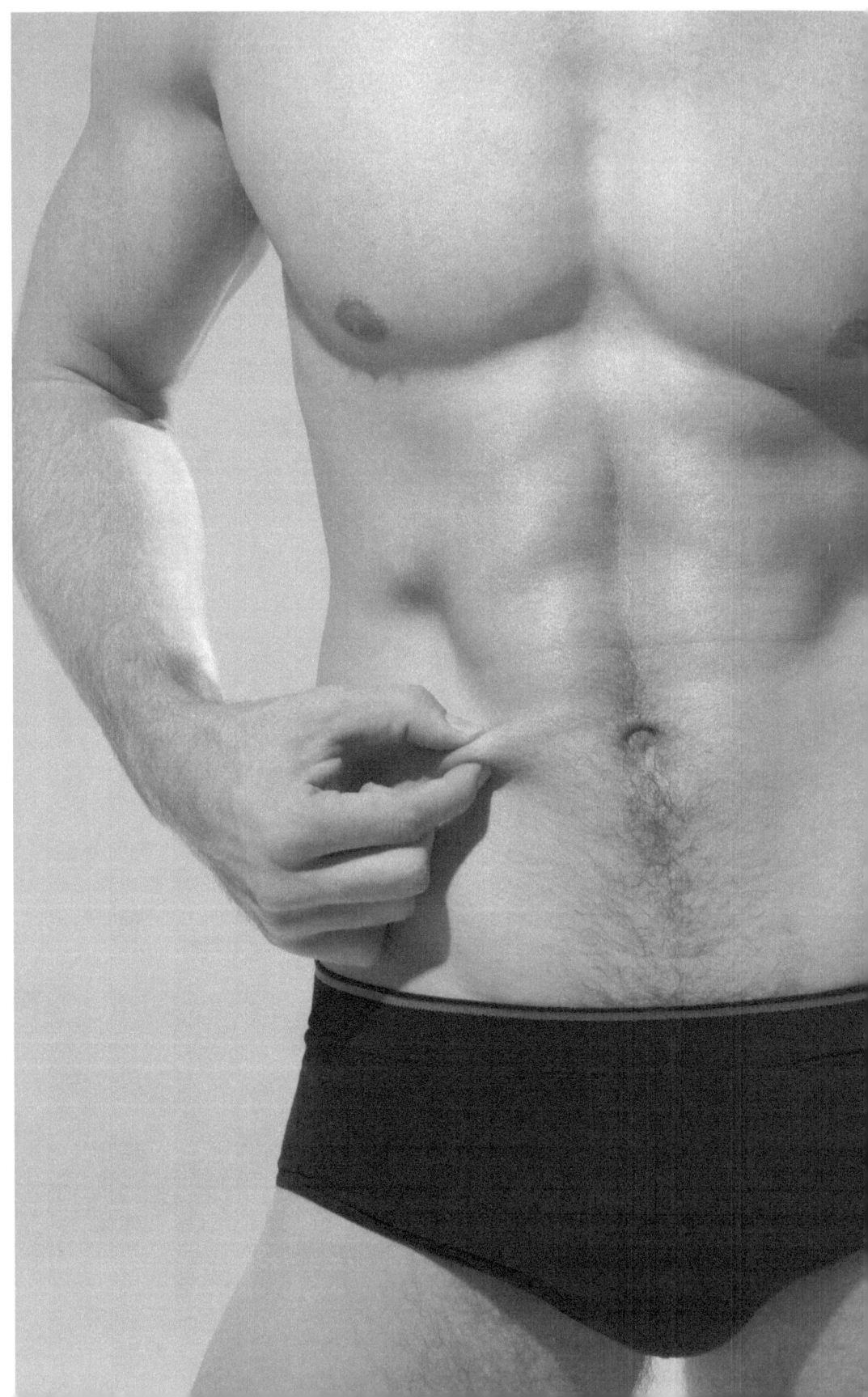

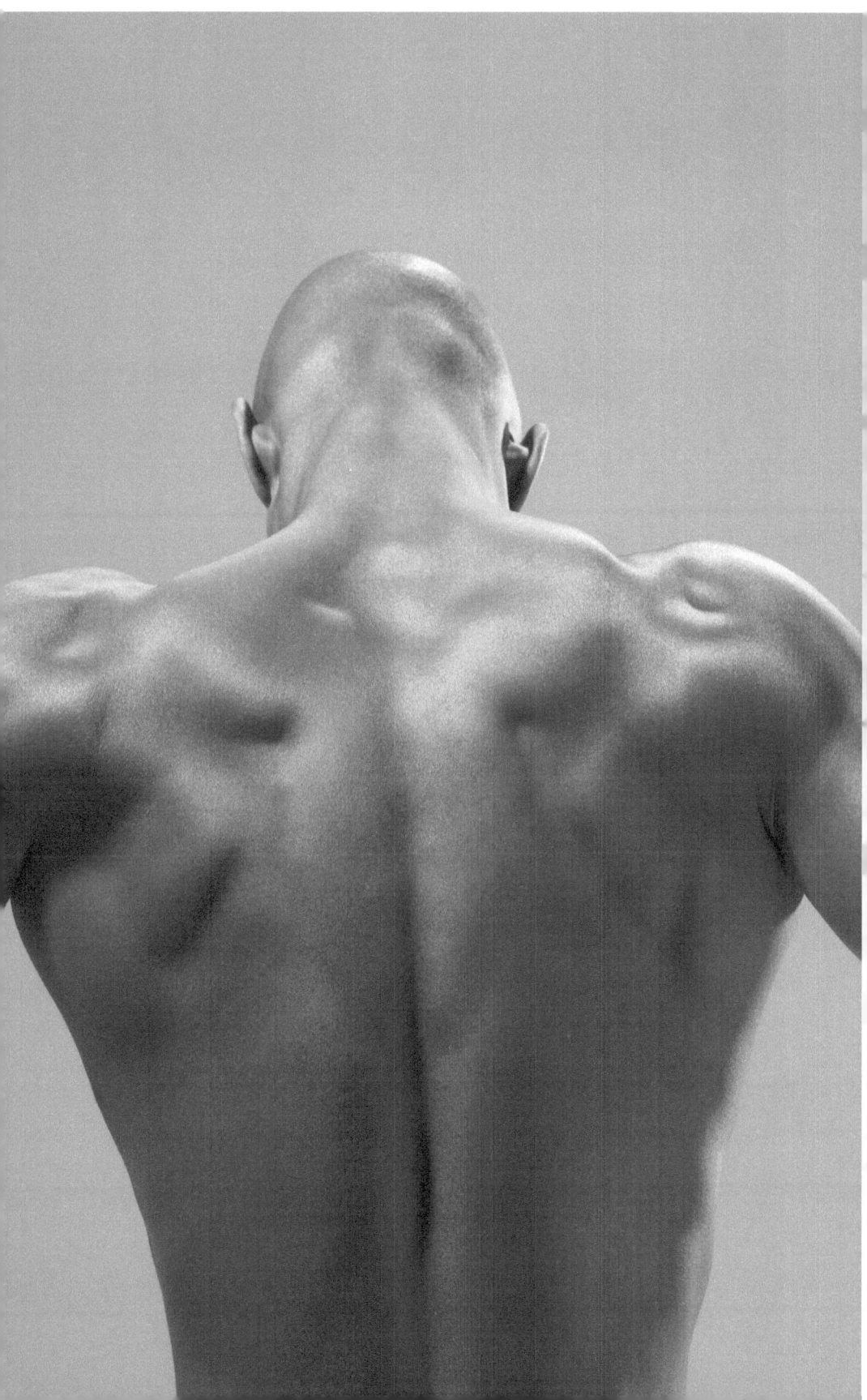

www.ingramcontent.com/pod-product-compliance
Lightning Source LLC
Chambersburg PA
CBHW030908180526
45163CB00004B/1750